Pennsylvania Vital Records Research

A Genealogy Research Guide for Birth, Adoption, Marriage, Divorce, and Death Records from the Colonial Era to Today

Denyse Allen

This publication is designed to provide accurate and authoritative information in regard to the subject matter covered. It is sold with the understanding that neither the author nor the publisher is engaged in rendering legal, investment, accounting or other professional services. While the publisher and author have used their best efforts in preparing this book, they make no representations or warranties with respect to the accuracy or completeness of the contents of this book and specifically disclaim any implied warranties of merchantability or fitness for a particular purpose. The advice and strategies contained herein may not be suitable for your situation. You should consult with a professional when appropriate. Neither the publisher nor the author shall be liable for any loss of profit or any other commercial damages, including but not limited to special, incidental, consequential, personal, or other damages.

Book Cover by Denys Allen

Images on front cover all taken by author on location in archives. Vital records from top to bottom: Marriage license application for Horace John Wilmer, Jr. and Mildred Anna John; Delayed birth certificate for John J. Wilmer,; Death certificate for John Wilmer.

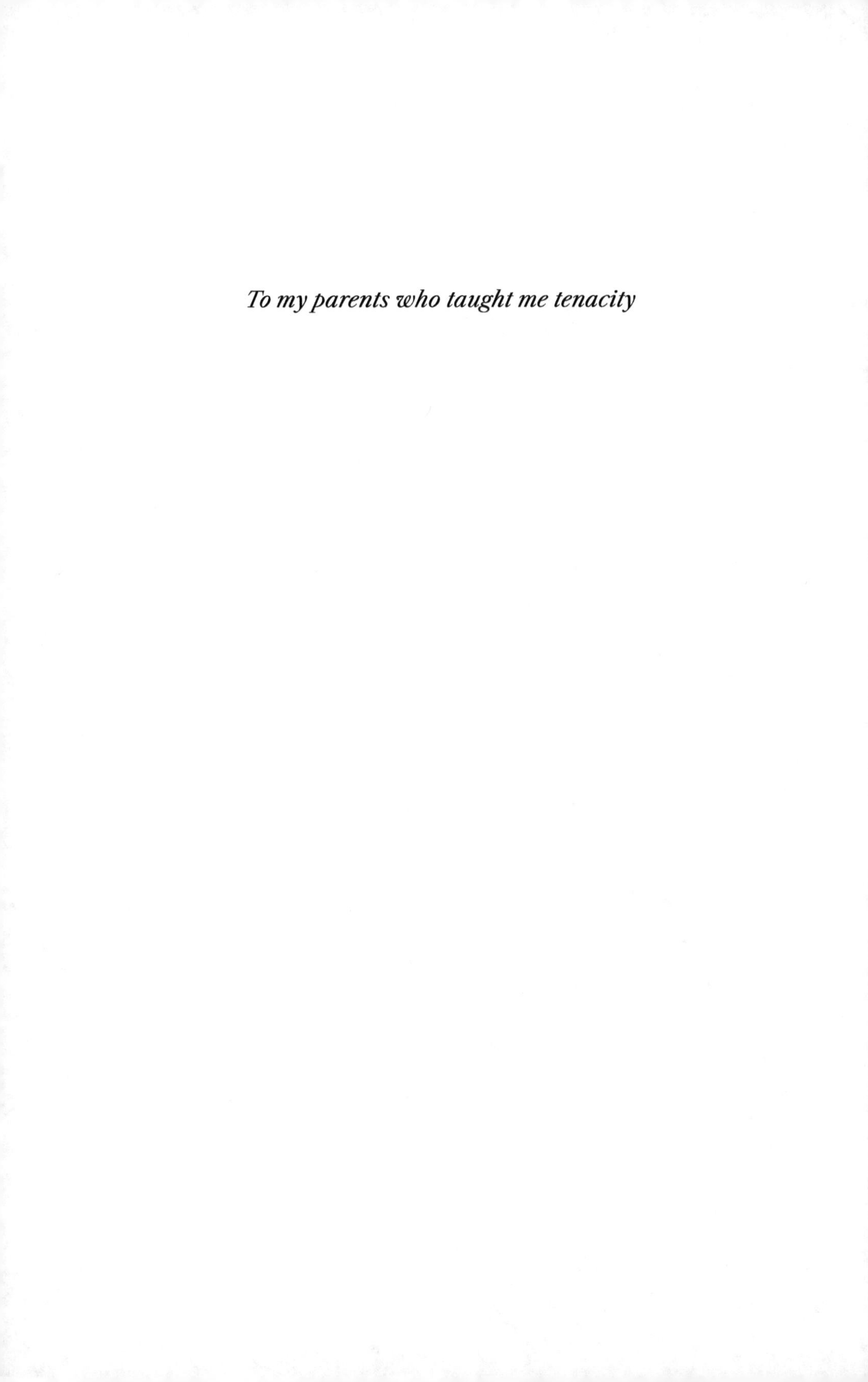

To my parents who taught me tenacity

Contents

Introduction

IN 2022 I DID not consider myself a writer. In 2024, I do.

Pennsylvania Vital Records Research was published in December 2022, and at that time getting the words I wanted on the page was a struggle. In the past 18 months I've written hundreds of thousands words about Pennsylvania and her records, and used ChatGPT to evaluate my writing and give me feedback. "Describe my writing style in this paragraph" and "Rewrite this paragraph into bullet points" are two prompts I used with artificial intelligence (AI). I do not use AI to write for me. I use AI as an infinitely patient writing coach to help me improve and finally feel comfortable writing.

This edition of the book was rewritten for clarity and style. The overall structure of the chapters and facts about each vital record remain unchanged. Explanations of records have been enhanced with images. The text was reformatted with Atticus for improved readability.

The majority of reviews for the original book have been very positive. If upon reading this version of the book you feel that it deserves less than 5 stars, please send me an email at hello@paancestors.com. Detail what I can provide in the text to make it 5 stars. I'd love to further improve the book for the genealogy community. We all grow together as genealogists when we publish books for others to use in their research.

Denyse Allen
June 2024

Original introduction:

Write the book you wish you had when you started.

That sentence above is the advice I received two years ago. I love genealogy, but I often wish that genealogy professionals would share more on *how* they researched. I could see from their citations *what* they researched, but I couldn't figure out how they knew that specific source existed. I knew they knew things about records that I did not know, but I didn't know what I didn't know.

I started making notes for myself. First, on what records were available, then, on where I could find them. In the beginning, I could rely on websites to guide me on what records were available for genealogy.

But soon I ran into complicated situations involving orphans, divorce, and unusual deaths. In order to understand those, I first needed to know what was "normal" at the time and what the law required. It was impossible to find the Pennsylvania laws and historical record keeping procedures in counties on websites.

And it was then that I realized there was not a website or a book that told me what I wanted to know. If I wanted to know more about vital records, maybe others did too.

During the covid shutdowns, I put in hundreds of hours of research with out-of-print books, archive staff, and, eventually, law libraries. I collected hundreds of pages of notes. Those notes became this book: *Pennsylvania Vital Records Research*. This book is the book I wish I had when I started doing Pennsylvania genealogy research. My hope is it become an valued resource in your Pennsylvania genealogy research.

Each chapter focuses on a type of vital record - birth, marriage, or death - or a record closely related to vital records - divorce, adoption, and DNA. The history, laws, and contents of the records are explained so family historians know what to expect. A guide and checklist on how to find each record is provided, so you know you've searched everywhere. The appendices include common terms found in vital records, resources to help locate records, and the actual vital record holders themselves (for anything not online).

While the history and past laws of vital records will not change, their access and locations absolutely will change. It's just a matter of when, not if. All website names, URLs, database titles, and physical addresses are correct as of December 2022. The book will be revised and updated when significant changes occur. Any errors or requested updates, can be sent to me through my website .

This is the first book I've written, and the process was made easier with the community of Write Useful Books, founded by Rob Fitz. A special shout-out to the Wednesday morning writing community who kept me motivated to keep going: Adam, Brian, Harry, Kate, John, and Marjorie. Part of the Write Useful Books process is involving Beta Readers early in the book writing process. Thank you to my Beta Readers - Anne, Christine, Debbie, Deborah, Karen, Kathleen, Lynn, Rebecca and Taerie - for their comments and feedback, and encouraging words. You all kept me going in the messy middle of this book. Gaynor Haliday edited the manuscript and her support meant more than she knows. Any errors or grammar oddities within these pages are all mine. Behind every writer is a supportive family, and my family is no different. Matt, Cassie, and Elle have listened to me talk about this book for a year and never once stopped believing I'd publish it, even when I doubted it myself.

Everything useful about vital records in Pennsylvania is in this book. Now you know everything I know! My wish is you make many new discoveries on your ancestors from what you learn here.

Denyse Allen
December 2022

Chapter 1

Getting Started in Pennsylvania Genealogy Research

FOR MANY FAMILY HISTORIANS, their first hint they have Pennsylvania ancestors is a notation on the census or a death certificate of "Birthplace: Penna."

Their next step is searching on one of the major genealogy websites for birth records. However, it soon becomes clear that research in the Keystone state is quite confounding! There are not as many birth, marriage, and death records as family historians assume there would be. Many of the historical vital records remain unindexed, and therefore, are not returned through search on genealogy websites. This book will cover in its chapters exactly where to find vital records and how to search for them.

But first, knowing how Pennsylvania is organized and having a approach to research in the state can help you get started, or re-started, on solid footing.

- Pennsylvania began in 1681 when William Penn received the charter for the land from England. Its first laws were issued in 1682.
- There are sixty-seven counties in the state now, including

the City of Philadelphia which was founded in 1854 from the boundaries of Philadelphia County. Some today say there are 66 counties plus the City of Philadelphia. The important part to remember is that both land and counties were added from 1682 to 1878. County boundary line changes are not covered in this book. See Appendix E:Additional Resources for Research for help with county boundary changes.

- Migration was difficult in a straight east–west direction across the state due to the Appalachian Mountains. There are also few rivers navigable by boat, and those run north–south. People migrating from the Philadelphia area typically went south to Maryland and Virginia, then north to get to the Pittsburgh area. Keep this in mind when tracing the movements of ancestors.

- County records are essential to vital records research, yet there is no central collection in the state of all county records. Pennsylvania's adjoining states of Delaware, Maryland, and New Jersey have moved most of their county records to their state archives. Pennsylvania has not done so due to the volume of county records. Many county records have been microfilmed over the years by the Utah Genealogical Association (now FamilySearch) but no county has a complete collection microfilmed and available through search online. Each chapter in the book provides checklists of how to search for each record type both online and offline. Artificial Intelligence (AI) holds the promise of indexing all records on microfilm in the near future, but until that happens, the research approach in this book works.

- Pennsylvania had, and continues to have, distinct regional differences: east to west, north to south, center to borders, and even county to county. Assuming people in one location kept their records in the exact same way as people in another location can trip up researchers. Record-keeping practices are similar across each record type, but there are differences by location and ethnicity, particularly the farther back one goes.

- Pennsylvania ethnic diversity is astounding. AncestryDNA counts eighty distinct genetic communities across the state. To use your autosomal DNA results with your vital records research, see Chapter 2: Using DNA Results in Vital Records Research. If you have not done a DNA test through Ancestry, you do not need it. In most cases you can complete your research successfully without it.

Now that you know this history and structure of Pennsylvania and its records, let's cover an approach for genealogical research that combines the power of genealogical websites and methods for analysis.

Suggested Research Approach

As was mentioned, there is little success in using the main search box on any genealogy website to find all the records you need. The approach I am suggesting here combines what is available online through search with some additional analysis on the researcher's part to find what is needed. Here are my four steps for successful genealogical research in Pennsylvania:

1. Begin at the end of a person's life and work backwards
2. Create your own databases of records
3. Collect vital records on every family member
4. Write about what you find as you research

Combine these four steps with the specific checklists at the end of each chapter for maximum results.

Begin at the end of a person's life and work backwards

Every biography and memoir starts with a person's birth, moves through to the events of his or her life, and ends with his or her death.

It is tempting to research in this order of birth to death, but it can create frustration and confusion. For most of our ancestors, state law required more records be created at the time of their death than when they were born. By starting at the end of a person's life where we have more records, we can gather the details that will help us locate the correct birth record.

Collect every record an ancestor made where he or she died. This includes their entire estate filing (also called probate records), property (deed) records, cemetery information, obituary, and anything related to their religious practices. Most of these records are county records and were filed at the county courthouse where that ancestor lived. County newspapers are not all online, so check with the local genealogical society on where to find more newspapers. In most counties there are eight to twenty newspapers available on microfilm.

Once these records are collected combine them with the census records you have and assemble the details into a timeline of that ancestor's life. You may want to also use maps to identify exact locations and family nearby. By the end of this assembly, you should have enough information to be able to pluck your ancestor out of a group of similarly named people based on what you know. (And chances are you will encounter many similarly named people while researching in Pennsylvania!)

Create your own databases of records

When you create your own database, you can ensure that you have a thorough listing of every person with a name similar to your ancestor, and an exact location where each person lives. Plus you will have a listing of every spelling variation of that surname.

First, let's cover surname spellings, then we will create a database.

Two factors confound genealogists researching anywhere: the number of people with similar names and the number of spelling variations for surnames. In the present day, we expect people to have one, and only one, spelling of their name. But for any time prior to about 1930, the spelling of a surname could vary from slightly to significantly. Genealogy websites often assist in showing additional records with similar sounding surnames or abbreviated spellings of given names. What can be helpful is to make your own list of the various ways you have found a surname spelled or use existing resources to intentionally misspell names to ensure no name is missed. See Appendix D: Additional Resources for Research for help with name variations.

Here's an example of the many ways a German ancestor of mine had his surname spelled on documents:

- "Streibach," 1860 U.S. census
- "Strwick," 1870 U.S. census
- "Streibig," 1880 U.S. census
- "Striebig," Philadelphia Death Certificate, 1887
- "Streibig," Union Army Pension File Index Cards
- "Streivish" and "Strinwich," Compiled Military Service Record for Union Army

Those are the variations for one man! His siblings and parents had even more spelling variations of their shared surname. It appears that my German-speaking family could not spell in English and simply said their name to clerks, who spelled what they heard. A common situation for many non-English speaking immigrants.

Additional spellings of "Streibig" were found as I collected records on all the Streibig's who lived in the area, Most of them were related to each other, so I simply added them to my family tree. I then copied and pasted each spelling I found into the top of my research log so I had a list of what to search in each new record collection.

Now we will cover how to create a database of records from genealogy websites.

Why create your own database of records? Having your own database allows you to methodically go through each record for your ancestor and make notes of your results. For example, in the censuses prior to 1850 only heads of households were listed by name, and no one else in the family. By creating your own database of a pre-1850 census, you can target your focus on households of the surname you need by specific locations. Each household can be checked for people that match the age of your ancestors, and those that do not can be eliminated. This process results in a small list of possible families for further research, rather than trying to tackle the entire state (or country) at once.

The two tools you need to create your own database are a spreadsheet program (Excel, Numbers, GoogleSheets) and a free account on FamilySearch.

In the example below, I will show how I built a database of all the Heberling's in the 1830 census in Pennsylvania. My research question is to find the parents of Joseph Heberling born around 1814 in Pennsylvania. I know from census records and the vital records of Joseph's children that he was born in Pennsylvania, but no county. I have used census and tax records to follow Joseph Heberling's life from 1868 back to 1836 in Ferguson Township, Centre County. There are no other Heberling families in Ferguson Township, so my goal is to find other Heberling households in Pennsylvania in 1830 where Joseph could have been born. To ensure I examine each Heberling household, I am going to create a database of 1830 census records.

1.On a desktop or laptop computer go to FamilySearch.com and log in. Using the main search box, type in your ancestor's surname in the surname field, and "Pennsylvania, X" in the location field. X is the county you wish to search if you have a county. If not, just type Pennsylvania for the location. No need to enter a birth year or death year and click Search.

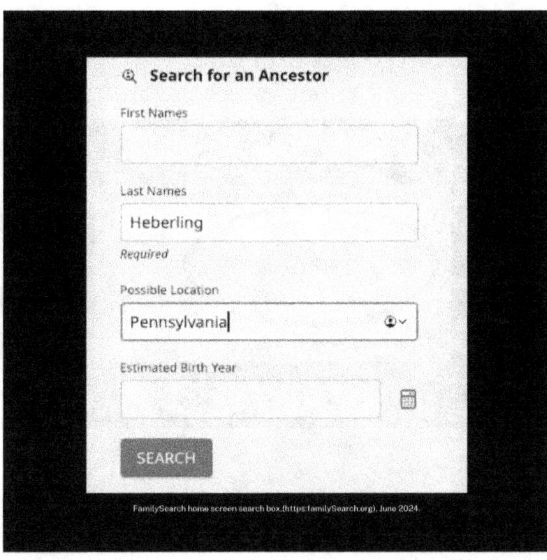

FamilySearch home screen search box.(https:familySearch.org). June 2024.

2. You will get thousands of results returned. Ignore them.

3. Look at the “Collections” in the side column. Choose the option for censuses.

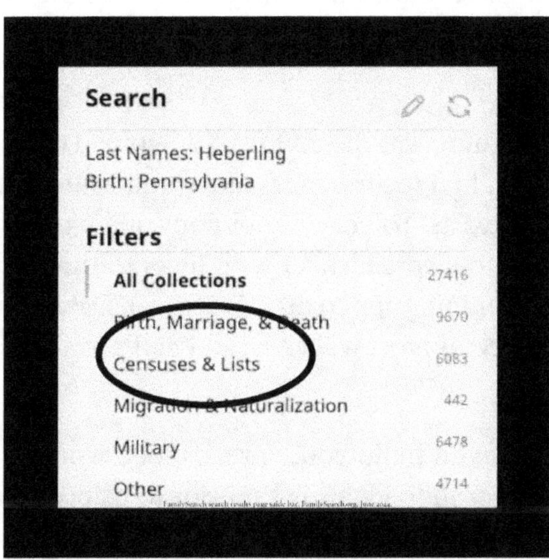

4. Scroll through the list until you see a census collection for the year

you want. For my Heberling example, I am using "United States Census, 1830". Click on this record collection title.

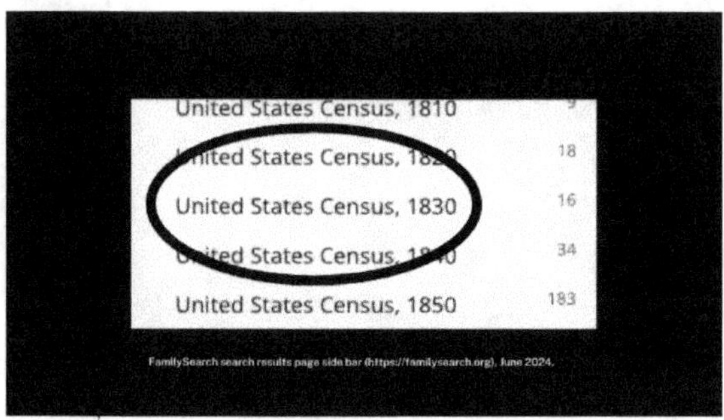

FamilySearch search results page side bar (https://familysearch.org), June 2024.

5. What you now have in the search screen is very focused list of all the heads of households with your ancestor's surname who lived in Pennsylvania at the time of that census. In this example with Heberling's in Pennsylvania in 1830, I have 16 households. A very focused and targeted search!

Note: FamilySearch is continually changing their website design so the images of the website shown here may not match the current website. However the steps involved of going from a broad search to a narrow one are the same.

Before June 2024 there was the ability to download these search results along with the attached record image as a spreadsheet file. Currently no download option exists. You can either copy and paste the information for each record into a spreadsheet with links to the image, or you can search for a data scraping app to do this for you. Data scraping is against the terms of service of most websites, so I can not advocate doing this, but it is possible.

Regardless of how you build your spreadsheet, working off a targeted list of households or individuals is superior to using the general search box. You will be able to methodically examine each household against what you know of the family and narrow your search to just those who meet your criteria. Plus by making notes of your search results along the way, your family members will be able to follow your research trail and understand how you reached the results you did.

Lastly, repeat the search and database building for each variation of the surname spelling you have. Usually genealogy websites assist in providing alternative spellings, but as I showed in the Streibig example above, some spellings are so far off the usual spelling variations, that they get missed.

Collect vital records on every family member

Because family members are born and die in different times and places, the types of records each one creates can vary in quality. For example, Philadelphia's Department of Health began keeping death records in 1860. Those records began as listings of each individual in a ledger book. By the mid-1870s it evolved to single forms per person. The city's form evolved again to something similar to state death certificates in 1904. With each change to Philadelphia's death records, more information was collected on the deceased. Your direct line ancestor may not have the information you seek on his or her vital records, but you could find it on a sibling's record.

Each chapter in this book will tell you specifically which vital records exist by year and where to find them. If vital records do not exist for a particular time period, a list of other record suggestions is in Chapter 10: Substitutes for Vital Records.

When collecting vital records, obtain an image of the original form. Do not settle for what comes up in computer search summary page or index listing. It really does matter for family history to have that photocopy image or digital image. Frequently genealogy websites just show parts of the birth, marriage, or death records at first. Click through to view images and download them to your computer. These original record images will have additional details such as doctors, hospitals or institutions, ministers, informants, or burial details. Through out the book when I refer to vital records, it is these original records (or their images) I am referencing.

Write about what you find as you research

Almost everyone skips this step. Most researchers stay stuck in "collecting records" thinking if they just keep searching online, everything will fall into place. What often happens is repeated searches, frustration, and mistakes.

Writing about what you find as you find it (or do not find it) prevents errors, and speeds up research. Writing encourages you to look closely at the records and put them in logical order. Once they are in order, you start noticing gaps between records or repetition in people and places. Connections and patterns previously hidden will be revealed.

Before launching into new research, take some time and make a listing of everything you have found so far. Put it all in a research log writing about the details in each document in one of the columns, or write it out in a Word document. Writing with pen and paper works too! Simply open a document image and write about the details of what there. Carefully read every field, every notation, and even the back of the form, then type it into your research log or Word document.

This step feels tedious and not useful, but most researchers find they make major breakthroughs in their research when they write. Details and patterns emerge as our brain examines the facts we have found so far. We also note what is missing and discover new avenues for research.

Once you have assembled what you have and written about it, it is time to begin your research in vital records.

Chapter 2

Using DNA Results in Vital Records Research

WITH THE EVER-GROWING POPULARITY of DNA tests for genealogy, many researchers are asking, "Can DNA test results help me find vital records on my ancestors?" Yes, but not in the way we have been led to believe in television ads.

The advertising for DNA tests leads people to believe that they can have an instant family tree arrive in their email. Simply spit into a tube and your genealogy is done for you! The reality is that DNA testers receive screen after screen of shared DNA matches with other testers which they then need to further analyze.

Then how do you use DNA results for genealogy research, specifically vital record research?

Your DNA test results can be used in three ways to help with your vital records research:

1. Confirming relationships between ancestors
2. Matching ethnicity results to vital records
3. Targeting research with genetic communities

The most useful DNA test results for genealogy purposes are currently offered by Ancestry, 23&Me, My Heritage, and FamilyTreeDNA. There are other companies, but these four have the largest databases of test results which are also updated frequently. Each of these companies provides in their results two things which can help genealogists:

- A list of other living people the tester shares DNA with; and
- An assessment of ethnicity, and for Ancestry, genetic communities.

Both types of testing results can be used with vital records research.

Confirming Relationships Between Ancestors

Sharing DNA with other DNA test takers means sharing a relationship to a common ancestor.

The majority of DNA testing utilized in genealogy is autosomal DNA testing, which is most effective within five generations from the test taker. This type of testing helps identify living relatives who share a common ancestor with the tester. The closer this common ancestor is in generations to the testers, the more DNA they share. The Shared cM Project on the DNA Painter website at **https://dnapainter.com/tools/sharedcmv4**, managed by Jonny Perl, regularly updates the expected shared DNA amounts between ancestral descendants, providing a reliable reference for genealogists.

Genealogists use the amounts of shared DNA to confirm relationships between ancestors also. To make effective use of autosomal DNA, family trees must be built back to four generations or more. Additionally, the family trees must be built down from the oldest ancestor to present day living people. This is challenging work, but it is these living people who are the DNA test takers. Studying the shared centimorgans between test takers and comparing it to the Shared cM Project data confirms relationships from and between ancestors. Diahan Southard's *Your DNA Guide* offers practical instructions on effectively using autosomal DNA matches along with shared centimorgans.

Once a relationship through DNA is revealed, a genealogist can work collaboratively to share and swap family history, including vital records.

Some caution on using DNA to confirm ancestral lines: It is possible to blow apart existing family trees with newly discovered relatives. DNA test results often do this today. DNA testers receive results which inform them of new cousins, siblings, and occasionally parents or grandparents. Be prepared for this type of result when doing DNA testing.

Matching Ethnicity Results to Vital Records

America is a nation of immigrants. Every ethnicity in the world is represented within America's borders today.

What is ethnicity? Ethnicity refers to shared ancestry, culture, religion, and/or nationality within a group of people. Multiple ethnicities are represented within a single race. For example, Pennsylvania's largest racial group is "White." Within that one group are the broad ethnicities German, Irish, English, Italian, and Polish (Pennsylvania's historically most numerous ethnicities.). Each of those broad ethnicities can be further broken down into the specific regions, cultures, and/or religions. For genealogists, knowing the ethnicity of ourselves or our closest relatives through DNA testing, can validate completed family trees or point a direction for future research.

Vitals records such as birth certificates, marriage license applications, and death certificates provided a racial group and birth place on their forms. Ethnicity may or may not have been specifically named, but the race category combined the birth location can help determine ethnicity. For example, a German person could be noted to be from Bavaria or Prussia. An Irish person from Donegal or Mayo. These locations often correlate to ethnicity regions shown in DNA tests.

It can be helpful for researchers to compare ethnicity results across DNA testing companies. Each company has a different pool of testers and therefore categorizes their ethnicity results in its own way. Your DNA does not change, but how it is described changes depending on who your DNA is compared with. Each company providing testing shares their methodology, or thinking, about how they represent ethnicity. Check each company's help information for "white papers" which are in-depth reports on methodology.

Targeting Research with Genetic Communities

For a nation as genetically diverse as America, AncestryDNA's genetic communities are extremely helpful for research.

A genetic community is created by the shared DNA of a group of AncestryDNA members who descend from a population of common ancestors. These common ancestors lived in the same place and time period together. A genetic community can span several states, or it can be as small as a part of a county. AncestryDNA is continually refining genetic communities, so people who have DNA test results with AncestryDNA will see their genetic communities change over time.

Pennsylvania's genetic communities started with about a dozen communities six years ago, and now number over eighty communities. Having DNA results showing a relationship to one of these genetic communities can focus your Pennsylvania research, especially if you have a common surname.

This is the current list of AncestryDNA genetic communities for Pennsylvania's historical population:

- Early Connecticut & New York Settlers
- Rhode Island, Southern New York, and Northeast Pennsylvania Settlers
- Southern Ontario, Northern New York & Northern Pennsylvania Settlers
- Early Pennsylvania Settlers
- Early Settlers of Central Pennsylvania
- Early Settlers of Eastern Pennsylvania

- Early Settlers of North-Central Pennsylvania
- Early Settlers of Western Pennsylvania
- Eastern Ohio River Valley & Northern Blue Ridge Mountains Settlers
- Southeast Pennsylvania & Northern Maryland Border Settlers
- Southern Pennsylvania & Amish Country, Ohio Settlers
- New Jersey & Eastern Pennsylvania Settlers
- Mid-Atlantic Settlers
- Philadelphia, South & Central Jersey Settlers
- Northern Mid-Atlantic Settlers
- Bradford County, Pennsylvania & Southern Tioga County, New York Settlers
- New Jersey, New York & Pennsylvania Border Settlers
- Northeast Pennsylvania Settlers
- Northeastern Pennsylvania & South-Central New York Border Settlers
- Southern New York & Northern Pennsylvania & New Jersey Settlers
- Southwestern New York & North Central Pennsylvania Settlers
- Pennsylvania, Eastern Ohio, Northern West Virginia & Maryland Settlers
- Adams County, Pennsylvania & Carroll County, Maryland Settlers
- Allegheny & Butler County, Pennsylvania Settlers
- Armstrong County, Pennsylvania Area Settlers

- Bedford, Blair & Huntingdon County, Pennsylvania Settlers
- Berks County, Pennsylvania Settlers
- Cameron & Eastern Elk County, Pennsylvania Settlers
- Central & Eastern Pennsylvania Settlers
- Central & Eastern Westmoreland County, Pennsylvania Settlers
- Central & Northern Lancaster County, Pennsylvania Settlers
- Central & Western Lancaster County, Pennsylvania Settlers
- Central Eastern West Virginia Settlers
- Central Pennsylvania Settlers
- Centre & Clearfield County, Pennsylvania Settlers
- Centre & Clinton County, Pennsylvania Settlers
- Clarion & Venango County, Pennsylvania Area Settlers
- Clearfield, Centre & Clinton County, Pennsylvania Border Settlers
- Clinton & Lycoming County Pennsylvania Settlers
- Columbia & Western Luzerne County, Pennsylvania Settlers
- Columbiana & Mahoning Counties, Ohio & Western Pennsylvania Border Settlers
- Dauphin, Cumberland, York & Adams County, Pennsylvania Settlers
- Eastern Allegheny & Westmoreland County, Pennsylvania Settlers
- Eastern Central Pennsylvania Settlers
- Eastern Centre & Southern Clinton County, Pennsylvania

Settlers

- Eastern Crawford & Western Warren County, Pennsylvania Settlers
- Eastern Jefferson & Western Clearfield County, Pennsylvania Settlers
- Eastern Mercer & Western Venango County, Pennsylvania Settlers
- Eastern Pennsylvania Settlers
- Eastern West Virginia & Northwestern Virginia Settlers
- Eastern West Virginia, Western Maryland & Northern Virginia Settlers
- Fayette & Westmoreland County, Pennsylvania Settlers
- Indiana County, Pennsylvania Settlers
- Jefferson, Clarion, & Armstrong County, Pennsylvania Border Settlers
- Lancaster County Area, Pennsylvania Settlers
- Lawrence & Beaver County, Pennsylvania Settlers
- Lawrence & Mercer County, Pennsylvania & Ohio Border Settlers
- Lebanon, Dauphin & Berks County, Pennsylvania Settlers
- Lycoming, Sullivan, Columbia & Luzerne County, Pennsylvania Settlers
- North Central Pennsylvania Settlers
- Northeastern West Virginia Settlers
- Northern Armstrong & Southern Clarion County, Pennsylvania

Settlers

- Northern Cambria County, Pennsylvania Settlers
- Northern Somerset County, Pennsylvania Settlers
- Northern Susquehanna River Settlers
- Northern West Virginia, Southeastern Ohio, & Southwestern Pennsylvania Border Settlers
- Northern West Virginia, Southern & Eastern Pennsylvania & Northern Maryland Settlers
- Northumberland County, Pennsylvania Settlers
- Northwestern Berks County, Pennsylvania Settlers
- Northwestern Cambria County, Pennsylvania Area Settlers
- Northwestern Pennsylvania Settlers
- Northwestern West Virginia Settlers
- Philadelphia, Pennsylvania Region Settlers
- Schuylkill & Northwestern Berks County, Pennsylvania Settlers
- South Central Pennsylvania & Northern Maryland Settlers
- South Central Pennsylvania & West Virginia Border Settlers
- Southeastern Berks County, Pennsylvania Settlers
- Southeastern Ohio Settlers
- Southeastern Pennsylvania Settlers
- Southern Armstrong & Northern Westmoreland County, Pennsylvania Settlers
- Southern Armstrong County, Pennsylvania Settlers

- Southern Bedford & Fulton County, Pennsylvania Settlers
- Southern Butler & Northern Beaver County, Pennsylvania Settlers
- Southern Central Pennsylvania & Northwestern Maryland Border Settlers
- Southern Central Pennsylvania Settlers
- Southern Huntingdon County, Pennsylvania Settlers
- Southern Somerset County, Pennsylvania & Western Maryland Border Settlers
- Southern Westmoreland County, Pennsylvania Settlers
- Southwestern Pennsylvania & Northern West Virginia Border Settlers
- Southwestern Pennsylvania & West Virginia Border Settlers
- Southwestern Pennsylvania Settlers
- Southwestern Pennsylvania Wilds Settlers
- West Central Pennsylvania Settlers
- West Central Westmoreland County, Pennsylvania Settlers
- West Virginia, Pennsylvania & Maryland Border Settlers
- Western & Central Pennsylvania Settlers
- Western Clearfield, Southwestern Jefferson & Northern Indiana County, Pennsylvania Settlers
- Western Maryland & Eastern West Virginia Settlers
- Western Maryland & Pennsylvania Border Settlers
- Western Maryland & Southern Pennsylvania Border Settlers

- Western Maryland Settlers
- Western Pennsylvania & Eastern Ohio Border Settlers
- York County, Pennsylvania & North Central Maryland Border Settlers

By mapping the genetic community location along with an ancestor's location noted in documents, genealogists get a confirmation that their research is correct.

When a genealogist has gaps in his or her family tree, the genetic community can provide a direction where he or she should focus. For example, an ancestor, aged 75, died in Ohio in 1870 giving their birthplace as only Pennsylvania. This ancestor was born around 1795 and in that time period there are no birth records issued by the Pennsylvania government. The next best record to use is a baptism done in infancy, because these records often note the date of birth or age of the infant. In order to effectively research in church records, a county needs to be identified first.

For example, a test taker studies his genetic community results, and the community "Schuylkill & Northwestern Berks County, Pennsylvania Settlers" is shown. This indicates that the DNA test taker shares DNA with other testers who can trace their ancestors to that geographic area. Research for further records on this ancestor can now be focused on Schuylkill County and the northwestern part of Berks County, rather than the entire state.

Due to the small amounts of shared chromosomes shared by test takers in a genetic community, researchers are advised to use additional family members' DNA to confirm their findings. Perhaps one descendant's DNA is not a match to a Pennsylvania genetic community, but another descendant's DNA is.

Anyone doing DNA testing for any reason is encouraged to read the terms and conditions and privacy policy with each company to know how the results are used, stored, and shared. There are few state and federal laws regulating DNA testing currently and things can change quickly in any direction in the future.

While DNA results will not provide instant access to vital records, the results will help confirm documentary research completed and focus future research.

Chapter 3

Death Certificates

History of Death Certificates

IN MOST OF HUMAN history, the focus of death records was on burial records. Clergy kept burial registers for their graveyards, and gravestones marked a person's final resting place.

It was only at the beginning of the industrial age in England, that tracking causes of death became important. Britain led the way with civil recording of deaths in 1837. Soon America began recording deaths too, but in a hodgepodge of methods undertaken by cities and counties (See Chapter 5: Local Registrations of Births, Marriages, and Deaths.). It was not until the twentieth century that state-issued, individual death certificates were legislated.

In Pennsylvania, the State Assembly formed the Department of Health (DOH) in 1905. The DOH developed the death certificate form and a standardized process to record deaths and submit certificates to local DOH registrars. On January 1, 1906, Pennsylvania death certificates were compulsory. Each person who died within Pennsylvania's borders received a certificate, even if the individual was unidentified. The process that began in 1906 is essentially the same now.

While it is difficult to believe, in the early days after the process began, there was not 100 percent compliance with the issuing death certificates. In rural areas or among the economically poor classes in cities, people died and were buried (or otherwise disposed of) and no record of their death was made at the time. State law imposed a fine of $100 and a misdemeanor charge with jail time for interfering in the creation and filing of death certificates.[1] Today we have better processes to match missing people with unidentified bodies, and of course, even more substantial fines and jail time.

Death certificates are an essential part of modern life. For the government, death certificates are the foundation of vital statistics, public health, epidemic disease awareness, and population counting. For families, death certificates initiate the distribution of the deceased's estate, and claims for insurance and death benefits. Genealogists also see death certificates as essential tool, even though these certificates were never intended for use in genealogical research.

Purpose of Death Certificates

When death certificates became state-wide law in 1906, the completed form was required by funeral home directors and cemeteries in order to bury or cremate the deceased. No death certificate meant no burial Many cities had had this requirement in place for decades, and the new law brought rural areas into alignment with them.

A death certificate was also required to begin distribution of the deceased's assets to heirs, just like today. This death certificate had to a certified death certificate, issued by the DOH. This same type of certificate is needed for Social Security Death Benefits, life insurance proceeds, and employer or military pension packages.

Death certificates issued by a coroner (or medical examiner in some jurisdictions today) indicate that an investigation into the death of the individual was conducted. This means that the death was considered "suspicious" or "not natural." The files of the coroner's investigation are considered public record and available to anyone, not just family relations. To obtain the coroner or medical examiner files, contact the county courthouse in the county where the person died.

Department of Health Death Certificate

Death certificate, John Wilmer no. 84954, 6 Aug 1929, RG 011 Department of Health, Vital Statistics, Pennsylvania State Archives, Harrisburg, PA.

Information Collected on Death Certificates

Below is the list of fields expected to be completed on death certificates. Most information collected remains similar from 1906 to the present day. Symbols have been added (see key below) for additions and changes over the years.

- Registration District and Area, along with Registered Number and File Number
- Place of Death (County, Township/Borough/City, Street and Ward)

- Length of Residence in City or Town Where Death Occurred*
- If Death Occurred in Hospital or Institution
- Length of Stay in Hospital or Institution+
- Usual Residence of the Deceased*
- Length of Residence in City or Town Where Death Occurred*
- If Foreign Born, How Long in U.S..? (Years, Months, Days)* – changed to Citizen of What Country?^
- Full Name of Deceased
- If U.S. Veteran, Complete Other Side of Certificate* – changed to: Was Deceased Ever in U.S. Armed Forces?^
- Social Security Number+
- Sex
- Color or Race
- Date of Birth (Month, Day, Year)
- Age (Years, Months, Days – changed to Years on Last Birthday^)
- Age if Less Than One Year^
- Age if Less Than One Day (Hours, Minutes)+
- Single (changed to: Never Married+), Married, Widowed, or Divorced
- If Married, Widowed, or Divorced, Husband or Wife's Name*
- Birthdate
- Birthplace (State or Country), City or Town*
- Name of Father

- Birthplace of Father (State or Country), City or Town*
- Maiden Name of Mother
- Birthplace of Mother (State or Country), City or Town*
- Occupation
- Trade, Profession or Particular Kind of Work*
- Industry of Business in Which Work Was Done*
- Date Deceased Last Worked at This Occupation*
- Total Time (Years) Spent in This Occupation*
- Informant Signature and Address
- File Date and Registrar Name
- Date of Death
- Time of Death*
- Certification of Attending to the Deceased, with dates and times*
- Attestation to Last Saw Alive, with dates and times*
- Cause of Death and Duration (changed to Onset*)
- Contributory Causes and Duration (changed to Onset*)
- Major Findings of Operation or Autopsy+
- Was Autopsy Performed Yes/No?^
- If Death Was Due to External Causes, Fill in the Following:+
- (Probably) Accident, Suicide, Homicide (Specify)
- Date of Occurrence
- Where Did Injury Occur?

- Did Injury Occur in or about Home, on Farm, in Industrial Place, or in Public Place?
- While at Work?
- Means of Injury?
- Signed by M.D. with Date and Address
- Place of Burial or Removal – changed to: Burial, Removal or Cremation and Date^
- Name of Cemetery or Crematory^
- Date of Burial
- Undertaker (changed to Funeral Home+) and Address
- Registrar Signature and Date*

Key to the changes in the Death Certificate form:

* added in 1937, + added in 1942, ^ added in 1950

Process to Complete Death Certificates

The process to create and finalize a single Department of Health issued death certificate involves family members, the funeral home, the county coroner, the doctor, the dentist (if the death occurred in their care), the local vital record registrar, and the DOH itself. A doctor or coroner initiates the death certificate immediately after the death, noting the time, place, and cause of death. Next, an informant provides the details of the deceased, such as parents' names, birthplace, occupation, and residence. This informant is usually a family member, although it could be a person little known to the deceased, such as medical staff. Funeral homes or undertakers usually work with the informant (family member) to complete this information. The funeral home completes what happened to the deceased remains: burial, cremation, or donation for medical study.

While all this seems like great information for the genealogist, one thing is important to note about the information provided by the informant: nothing is verified. In other words, a family member does not need to provide documents showing who the decedent's parents were, nor where and when the deceased was born. The information provided can be completely true and easily corroborated with other documents, completely false, or somewhere in-between.

This can sound ridiculous to say, but no dead person provides the information for his or her own death certificate ahead of time. Whatever is reported on the form is what other people knew about that person, not what the person knew about himself or herself. Genealogists must always correlate the information on death certificates with other records.

What do the numerical codes on death certificates mean?

Every death certificate is annotated with numerical or numerical/alphabetical codes in the "cause of death" section. These 3- or 4-digit codes refer to the International Classification of Diseases (ICD) database currently maintained by the Center for Disease Control and Prevention in Atlanta, Georgia.

This method of categorizing deaths by their causes was developed in the late 1800s in France. It was known for a time as the International List of Causes of Death. ICD codes were used in countless other countries before the United States adopted it in 1898. ICD codes assist in easy compilation of vital statistics, by categorizing and counting the numbers of people who died from each cause.

If a genealogist is unable to read the cause of death on a death certificate, he or she can check for this number or number/letter code. This code on death certificates prior to 1970 is hand written in blue or red pencil.

Note: It is important to use the ICD code list available at the time of death. For example, if the 2010 ICD code list is used on a 1920 death certificate, wrong conclusions will be reached. An online resource for historical ICD codes is the website Wolfbane Cybernetics at **http://www.wolfbane.com/icd/**.

How to Find Death Certificates

Recent Pennsylvania Death Certificates (those issued within the last fifty years) are only available to immediate family members. Requests for these are made directly to the PA DOH for certified copies. Visit the DOH website **https://www.health.pa.gov/** for details on ordering, pricing, and any requirements.

Death certificates dated 51 years or older are considered public records. Public records in Pennsylvania are available to anyone, with no restrictions. Each year the newly public original death certificates are physically moved in boxes from the PA DOH offices to the PA State Archives for public access.

Once the original certificates have been moved to the PA State Archives in Harrisburg, Ancestry employees scan each certificate to create a digital image. These digital images are then indexed by the decedent's name, date of death and location, date of birth and location, parents' names, and certificate number. The digitization and indexing process can take years to complete.

Here is the schedule for the next six years of certificate transfers from the DOH to the Archives:

Death Certificate Availability

Year of Death	Available in Archives
1906-1972	2024
1973	2025
1974	2026
1975	2027
1976	2028
1977	2029
1978	2030

Death certificate images are viewable on Ancestry in the collection "Pennsylvania Death Certificates, 1906–1970," found at: **https://www.ancestry.com/search/collections/5164/**. (**Note:** The title of this database changes as it is updated with additional years of certificates. The website URL, however, remains the same.)

This collection is special among Ancestry collections in that it consists of high resolution, full-color digital images. Most genealogy records are in black and white only, because they are digitized from microfilm. Genealogy researchers are able to see every ink color, stray mark, and even notes in the margins and on the back of the forms. Not every certificate has writing on the back, but be sure to look by navigating to the next image in the database.

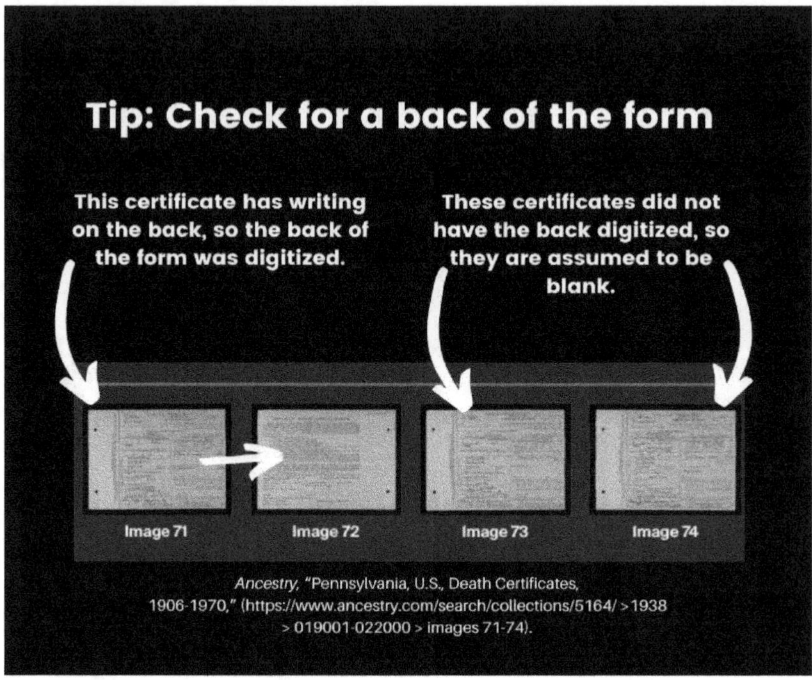

Ancestry, "Pennsylvania, U.S., Death Certificates, 1906-1970," (https://www.ancestry.com/search/collections/5164/ >1938 > 019001-022000 > images 71-74).

Checklist for Searching

- To assist in the search as you go, be sure to use variations of the spelling of the first name and surname. Keep a list of the variations you use so you search consistently.
- As of June 2024, Ancestry hosts full-color digitized copies of Pennsylvania's publicly available state death certificates. The collection is searched by entering the surname and first name of the deceased, and county, if known. The database is found at **https://www.ancestry.com/search/collections/5164**
- If your search returns no useful results, use the original PA DOH indexes at the PA State Archives **https://www.phmc.pa.gov/archives** under the Vital Statistics menu. These indexes are organized by year of death, then alphabetical by last name. In the final column is the certificate

number for each individual recorded. Use the certificate number to search the Ancestry database by entering the number in the "Certificate Number" field.

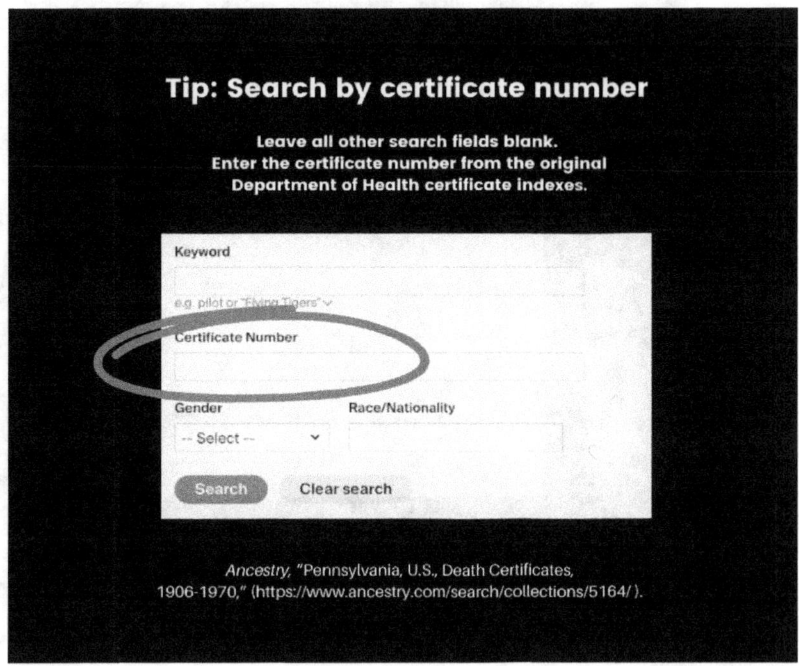

Ancestry, "Pennsylvania, U.S., Death Certificates, 1906-1970," (https://www.ancestry.com/search/collections/5164/).

- If a death certificate is not found in the DOH index, it's possible the person died outside of Pennsylvania. Death certificates are created in the jurisdiction where the person died. For example, if your ancestor went to the Jersey Shore and was attacked by a shark and died, his death certificate would be issued by the New Jersey Department of Health and archived there. Obituaries and local newspaper articles could provide clues as to a place of death outside of the Pennsylvania. Many genealogical societies have indexes of obituaries from all local newspapers in their county. (Only a small percentage of local papers are digitally available for Pennsylvania.)

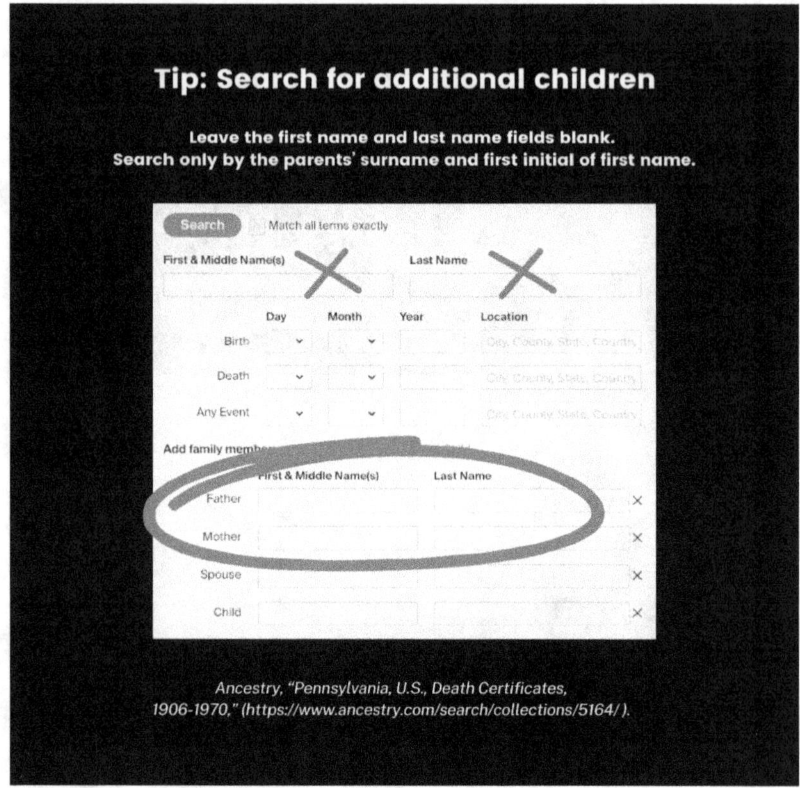

Ancestry, "Pennsylvania, U.S., Death Certificates, 1906-1970," (https://www.ancestry.com/search/collections/5164/).

- To gather additional information on your target ancestor, search for all the death certificates of his or her children. The death rate for infants and children under five years old was as high as 20 percent in the twentieth century.[2] Each child who died was issued a death certificate, and the parents almost always provided the information about the child and themselves. The recorded parent information, such as maiden surname and birth places, are different each time. To search on Ancestry for all children of a couple, leave the top main name field blank. Enter only the father's name and/or mother's name in the search fields. Your search will give you a short list of children born to parents with those names. Many researchers find at least one new child using this method.
- Be sure to collect the death certificates for all the siblings of

the deceased. Informants probably varied across the certificates, and each one reported the names and birth places of the parents in a different way. It can be helpful to create a table of the information gathered to better analyze it.

Book Bonus: To help you in your vital records research, I have created a free research plan template you can download. Go to **https://www.paancestors.com/book-bonuses/**to get it.

---

1. Act No. 218 of April 27, 1905. See Appendix B for a listing of Pennsylvania state laws on vital records.

2. Guyer, Bernard, et.al., "Annual Summary of Vital Statistics: Trends in the Health of Americans During the 20th Century," *Pediatrics*, Volume 106, Issue 6, American Academy of Pediatrics.

Chapter 4

Birth Certificates

History of Birth Certificates

THE HISTORY OF STATE-ISSUED birth certificates is similar to death certificates. Both vital records came into law together in 1906, and both were (and still are) managed by the same state government agency, the Pennsylvania Department of Health (DOH).

However, birth certificates were less likely to be completed and submitted to local registrars than death certificates. A study conducted by the U.S. Census Bureau comparing census counts to state birth certificate submissions, showed the completion rate was 96.4 percent in 1950.[1] It is not known exactly which newborns did not receive birth certificates between 1906 and 1950. We only the number of newborns from comparing the number of birth certificates issued to the count of infants on the 1950 Census. For genealogists, this means they may be searching for a birth certificate that was never created.

Doctors and midwives were required by law to complete a birth certificate for each child born in their care. What kind of factors affected compliance with the law? Factors such as economic class, race, ethnicity, and English language fluency have been studied as possible reasons. Children born outside of marriage were also more likely to not have a birth certificate issued. It's also possible that mothers had family or friends assist with the birth of their babies and no doctor of midwife was present to complete the birth certificate. (All of these reasons for lack of compliance to birth certificates, also apply to lack of compliance for birth registrations covered in the next chapter.)

Purpose of Birth Certificates

While the DOH wanted a birth certificate filed for each baby born in the state, parents and children had no purpose for the birth certificate itself. There was no universal need for individuals in 1906 to have a birth certificate for personal identification. If a person needed to confirm their identity, it was done through the use of sworn affidavits, not birth certificates.

To increase compliance with the issuance of birth certificates, the state paid counties 50 cents per certificate submitted to local registrars beginning in the 1920s.[2] Local registrars then followed up with doctors and midwives who did not comply with the law. The state government also created a new use for birth certificates around the same time: public school registration. By the 1930s, adults needed birth certificates to register for Social Security and military service. The federal government also made state birth certificates necessary to prove U.S. citizenship, and a necessary step for paid employment at the time.

Today it is impossible to live in American society without a birth certificate. Birth certificates are an essential part of one's identity. They are used to register for a social security number, obtain a driver's license or state identification card, obtain a U.S. passport, enroll in schools, and enlist into the military.

The DOH used birth certificates, like their predecessor birth registrations, to tabulate vital statistics and assess public health. Two measures of public health were (and are) their focus: lowering infant mortality rates, and assessing and preventing communicable diseases. Infants and young children are often most affected by disease outbreaks and tracking their births and deaths are a useful health metric.

The other current function of birth certificates is in population projections. The Census Bureau collects each state's birth statistics, compiles them with its own data, and shares the findings freely. Corporations such as baby food and children's toy manufacturers use it to plan production. States use the data to plan school buildings and housing. Counties and cities also allocate government resources to help in areas suffering from issues such as infant prematurity and higher child mortality.

Department of Health Birth Certificate

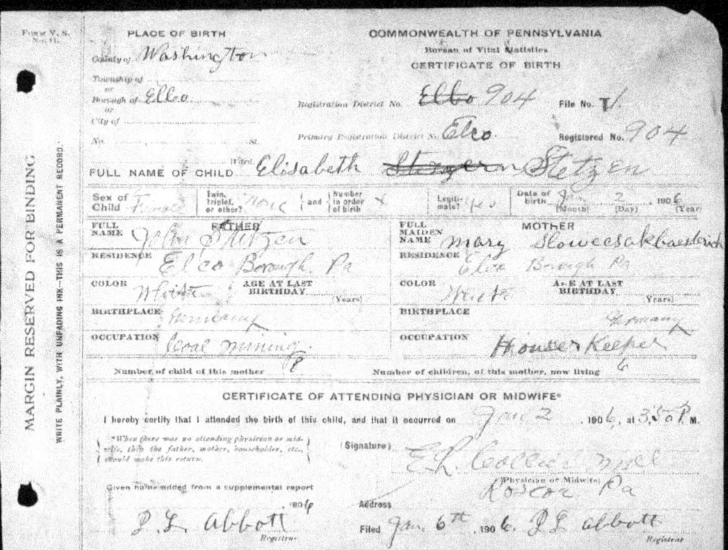
MARGIN RESERVED FOR BINDING
WRITE PLAINLY, WITH UNFADING INK—THIS IS A PERMANENT RECORD.

PLACE OF BIRTH

COMMONWEALTH OF PENNSYLVANIA
Bureau of Vital Statistics
CERTIFICATE OF BIRTH

County of Washington
Township of or Borough of Ellco or City of
Registration District No. Ellco 904 File No. 1
Primary Registration District No. Ellco Registered No. 904
No. St. Ward.

FULL NAME OF CHILD Elisabeth ~~Stezeran~~ Stetzen

Sex of Child Female | Twin, triplet, or other? None | and Number in order of birth X | Legitimate? Yes | Date of birth Jan. 2 1906 (Month) (Day) (Year)

FATHER		MOTHER	
FULL NAME	John Stetzen	FULL MAIDEN NAME	Mary Slowecsak
RESIDENCE	Ellco Borough Pa	RESIDENCE	Ellco Borough Pa
COLOR	White	COLOR	White
AGE AT LAST BIRTHDAY	(Years)	AGE AT LAST BIRTHDAY	(Years)
BIRTHPLACE	Germany	BIRTHPLACE	Germany
OCCUPATION	Coal mining	OCCUPATION	House Keeper

Number of child of this mother 8 Number of children, of this mother, now living 6

CERTIFICATE OF ATTENDING PHYSICIAN OR MIDWIFE*

I hereby certify that I attended the birth of this child, and that it occurred on Jan 2 1906, at 3:50 P.M.

*When there was no attending physician or midwife, then the father, mother, householder, etc., should make this return.

(Signature) E. L. Colleen ...
(Physician or Midwife)
Address Roscoe Pa

Given name added from a supplemental report 1906
P. L. Abbott Registrar

Filed Jan. 6th, 1906. P. L. Abbott Registrar

Birth certificate, Elisabeth Stetzer, no.1, 2 Jan 1906, RG 011 Department of Health, Vital Statistics, Pennsylvania State Archives, Harrisburg, PA.

Information Collected on Birth Certificates

Initially, birth certificates were simple forms with fewer than a dozen fields. By the 1950s the certificates had expanded to include information on the health of both mother and baby. This medical data is sent to various state and federal agencies and used in statistics and studies. The medical information is not provided to individuals when they request copies of their own birth certificate today. Perhaps when those 1950s certificates become public record beginning in 2055, genealogists will have access to them.

The state birth certificates genealogists can access (including one's own) contain basic demographic information. This is a list of fields:

- Place of Birth: County and Township, Borough, or City
- Full Name of Child
- Color/Race
- Sex
- Twin, Triplet, or Other? (completed or left blank)
- Number in Order of Birth
- Legitimate? (answered "yes" or "no")
- Date of Birth
- Father's Full Name, Residence, Color/Race, Age, Birthplace, Occupation
- Mother's Full Maiden Name, Residence, Color/Race, Age, Birthplace, Occupation
- Number of Child of This Mother (Example: 1st, 2nd, 3rd, etc.)
- Number of Children of This Mother Still Alive
- Physician Name/Signature, Address and Date
- Registrar Name and Date

Pennsylvania state law assumes that the spouse or partner of the birth mother is the father of the child. Now with DNA testing we can verify this information and know that this is not necessarily true. In the past, an unmarried woman giving birth would not always provide a father's name. Today single women must provide a father's name, and this is verified with DNA testing as needed.

What are delayed birth certificates?

When the federal Social Security program began in 1939, working adults applying to the retirement program needed proof of their age. Adults who did not have a state birth certificate, a county/city birth registration, or a baptismal record showing their birth date, could file for a delayed birth certificate.

Delayed Birth Certificate (front)

O. C. Form No. 16 - 41

This is to certify that the following is a true and correct copy of a Delayed Special Birth Certificate, filed in the Orphans' Court of Montgomery County, as directed by Act 154 of the General Assembly, 1941.

(SEAL) Asst. Clerk of Orphans' Court

Form - HVS - DBCSR
Filed in accordance with Act 154, 1941

COMMONWEALTH OF PENNSYLVANIA
County of Montgomery
DELAYED BIRTH CERTIFICATE
SPECIAL REGISTRATION

File No. ....
Registered No. 3133
Filing Date Feb. 24, 1950
Date of Issuance ....

Full Name (type or print) John J. Wilmer — Sex male

Date of Birth September 17, 1876 (Month (by name), Day, Year)

Twin or triplet .... If so - born 1st, 2nd, 3rd .... Was mother married to father of child? Yes

PLACE OF BIRTH
County Montgomery
City—Boro—Town—Village—Township Plymouth Twp.
If hospital—give name and address home

Children born to this mother:
A. Children born alive and living at time of this birth, including this child 3
B. Previous children born alive but dead at time of this birth 2
C. Previous children born dead (stillborn) ....
Total number including this birth add A - B - C 5

FATHER OF CHILD
Full name John Wilmer
Color or race white Age at time of this birth 35 yrs.
Birthplace Sharon Hill (City, town, or county) Penna. (State or foreign country)
Occupation farmer
Present address deceased

If attending Physician or Midwife are still living have them sign here
Attendant at Birth Dr. Beaver (Specify if M. D., Midwife or Other)
Date signed .... 19..
Address
If deceased — so state deceased

MOTHER OF CHILD
Full name Martha Boggs Wilmer
Color or race white Age at time of this birth 30 yrs.
Birthplace Whitemarsh (City, town, or county) Penna. (State or foreign country)
Occupation housewife
Present address deceased

I John J. Wilmer, being first duly sworn on oath, testify that the facts concerning my birth set forth upon this application are true and correct.

John Wilmer
Signature of applicant

927 W. Washington St., Norristown, Pa.
Present address of applicant

I Certify that the above applicant for registration of facts of birth has appeared before me and testified to their truth as set forth and affixed his (his or her) signature thereto and in my presence

this 8th day of Feb. 1950

(SEAL)

Elizabeth R. Fox
Signature of Notary Public

Norristown, Pa.
Address of Notary Public

NOTARY PUBLIC My Commission expires April 27, 1953

Delayed birth certificate, John J. Wilmer, 24 Feb 1950, microfilm, Montgomery County Archives, Eagleville, PA.

A delayed birth certificate could be obtained by an adult by application, beginning in 1941. An adult would apply for himself or herself by submitting a multiple page form (Be sure to get all pages!). Information collected on applications includes:

- Full Name at Birth
- Place of Birth: County and Township, Borough, or City
- Date of Birth
- Color/Race
- Sex
- Twin, Triplet, or Other? (completed or left blank)
- Number in Order of Birth
- Legitimate? (answered "yes" or "no")
- Father's Full Name, Residence, Color/Race, Age, Birthplace, Occupation
- Mother's Full Maiden Name, Residence, Color/Race, Age, Birthplace, Occupation
- Doctor, Nurse, or Midwife Present at Birth
- Clergyman Present at Baptism
- Three Individual Affidavits with Relationship to the Applicant
- Full school and work history (in some counties)

Delayed Birth Certificate (back)

Delayed birth certificate, John J. Wilmer, 24 Feb 1950, microfilm, Montgomery County Archives, Eagleville, PA.

The applications were submitted either to the county Orphans' Court or to the Pennsylvania Department of Health (DOH). Each county and the DOH had its own variation of the form and the questions asked; there's no one standard delayed birth certificate application in the state. Pennsylvania's counties collected delayed birth certificates from adults from 1941 through to 1976. The DOH continues to accept submission of the forms today, although it is mostly used for infants, not adults.

If an ancestor completed a delayed birth certificate, the researcher is in for a treat. The depth and breadth of information collected is more helpful compared to standard infant birth certificates. Adult applicants selected their closest friends and family to provide affidavits, and gave the name of their religious leader, who could be different than the one at marriage or death. Infant birth certificates provide none of this information.

Process to Complete Birth Certificates

Birth certificates are primarily completed and filed by the physician or midwife present at time of birth. He or she completes the date, time, and place of birth of the infant. The remaining information on a birth certificate – name of the child, parents' names and birthplaces, and home address – is provided by an informant to the doctor or midwife. The preferred informant is the mother. If the mother is unable to provide the information, then the father is asked to provide it. If neither parent is able, then the informant is another relative, or lastly, hospital personnel. The informant signs the birth certificate form verifying that all information provided, including spellings, is correct.

Several weeks after the birth, the parent(s) of the child receives one copy of the certificate in the mail from the DOH. Parents have the option to correct spelling errors within a year of the child's birth. After a year, spelling corrections are considered 'name changes' and are processed through the family's local county Prothonotary at the courthouse.

How to Find Birth Certificates

Birth certificates issued within the last 105 years are only available to the individual named on the certificate, or immediate family members who are acting in a parental or guardian capacity. Requests for these certificates issued on or after January 1, 1919 (as of 2024), are made directly to the PA DOH for certified copies. Visit the DOH website at **https://www.health.pa.gov/** for details on ordering, pricing, and any identification requirements.

When a birth certificate is over 105 years old, it becomes a public record. Public records in Pennsylvania are available to anyone, with no restrictions. Each year the newly public original birth certificates are physically moved in boxes from the PA DOH offices to the PA State Archives for public access.

Here is the schedule for the next six years of transfers from the DOH to the Archives:

Birth Certificate Availability

Year of Birth	Available in Archives
1906-1918	2024
1919	2025
1920	2026
1921	2027
1922	2028
1923	2029
1924	2030

Once at the Archives, Ancestry employees make digital images of each certificate. These are then indexed in the collection, "Pennsylvania Birth Certificates, 1906–1914," found at **https://www.ancestry.com/search/collections/60484/**. (**Note:** The title of this database changes as it is updated with additional years of certificates. The website URL, however, remains the same.)

Keep in mind that the digitizing and indexing of these certificates can take years to complete after they become public records. Researchers can always contact the PA State Archives directly for publicly available birth certificates. Access to the digital image of the record through Ancestry is convenient, but not the only way to obtain a copy of the certificate.

How to find delayed birth certificates

The majority of delayed birth certificate applications received by counties from 1941 to 1976 are still in county courthouses. Pennsylvania had sixty-seven counties when these were created, but only about half of the counties' certificates have been microfilmed and digitized. The images of these thirty-five counties are on FamilySearch in the collection "Pennsylvania Delayed Birth Records, 1941-1976," found at **https://www.familysearch.org/search/collection/3743274**. County-filed delayed birth certificates that are not available through FamilySearch are in the Orphans' Court records. It is mostly likely the Orphans' Court in the county where the adult lived at the time he or she filed, but Pennsylvania residents could apply to any county Orphans' Court. Adults could also apply directly to the DOH beginning in 1941 for delayed birth certificates. Delayed birth certificate applications sent to the DOH were filed under the year of birth of that adult, alongside the standard birth certificates issued to infants.

Note: The years 1941 to 1976 used in describing delayed birth certificate county collections, refers to the time period adults applied for the certificates, not the birth years of the individuals.

Checklist for Searching

- To assist in the search as you go, be sure to use variations of the spelling of the first name and surname. Keep a list of the variations you use so you search consistently.

- Estimate the year of birth from age on census records, or use the birth year given (depending on the census year). Start the search by adding one year to either side of estimated birth year. For example, if a person provided a birth year of 1911 in the census, check for a birth certificate from 1910 through 1912. People in the past have been known to provide birth years as much as ten years apart across records, so, you may need to widen the search years as you go.

- As of June 2024, Ancestry hosts full-color digitized copies of publicly available state birth certificates. The collection is frequently searched by entering the surname and first name of the child, and county, if known. The database is found at **https://www.ancestry.com/search/collections/60484,** entitled "Pennsylvania, U.S., Birth Certificates, 1906-1914."

Ancestry, "Pennsylvania, U.S., Birth Certificates, 1906-1914," (https://www.ancestry.com/search/collections/5164/).

- If your Ancestry search returns no useful results or the certificate is not digitized yet, use the original PA DOH indexes at the PA State Archives at **https://www.phmc.pa.gov/archives**, under the Vital Statistics menu. These indexes are organized by year of birth, then alphabetical by last name. In the final column is the certificate number for each individual recorded. Use the certificate number to browse the Ancestry database by choosing the "Year", then the certificate number range and scrolling through to the one you want. Or simply add it to the "Keyword" field to get a list of certificates that share that number.

- If a birth certificate is not found in the DOH index, it is possible the person was born outside of Pennsylvania. Check the death certificate and/or obituary for clues. It's also possible that a birth certificate was not filed at the time of birth, so check for with the county Orphans' Court for a delayed birth certificate.

- If a child was adopted, the original birth certificate would have been amended with the adoptive parents' name. See Chapter 9: Unexpected and Unknown Parentage for additional clues in birth certificates for adoptees.

- Be sure to collect the birth certificates for all the siblings and cousins of the target ancestor. Information probably varied across the certificates, and parents' names and birth places reported differently each time. Most researchers have success in finding sought after information using this method.

- It is also worth verifying you have not missed any children born to the parents. It is possible a child was born to a couple, and that child died or was adopted out of the family between censuses. To search for children born to a couple, only enter the parents' names, and no child name in the main search box.

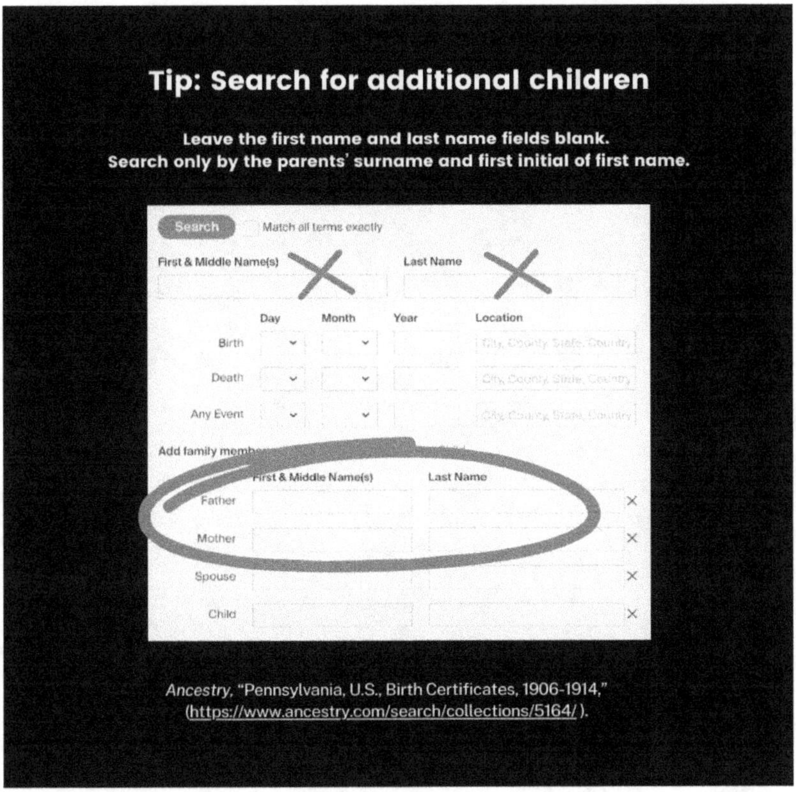
Tip: Search for additional children
Leave the first name and last name fields blank.
Search only by the parents' surname and first initial of first name.
Search
Match all terms exactly
First & Middle Name(s)
Last Name
Day
Month
Year
Location
Birth
Death
Any Event
Add family members
First & Middle Name(s)
Last Name
Father
Mother
Spouse
Child

Ancestry, "Pennsylvania, U.S., Birth Certificates, 1906-1914," (https://www.ancestry.com/search/collections/5164/).

Book Bonus: To help you in your vital records research, I have created a free research plan template you can download. Go to **https://www.paancestors.com/book-bonuses/**to get it.

---

1. Kluskens, Claire, "1950 Census: Infant Cards and the Special Infant Enumeration Study." 19 Apr 2021, *History Hub* (https://historyhub.history.gov/genealogy/census-records/b/census-blog/posts/1950-census-infant-cards-and-the-special-infant-enumeration-study).
2. Stevens, Sylvester K. and Kent, Donald H., *County Government and Archives in Pennsylvania*, p.79.

Chapter 5

Local Registrations of Birth, Marriage, and Death

History of Vital Record Registrations

PRIOR TO PENNSYLVANIA ISSUING birth and death certificates through the Department of Health, counties and large cities conducted registration of births, marriages, and deaths. These vital record registrations used a variety of forms and were implemented in different ways over the nineteenth century. It is confusing and contradictory time period, and this chapter will lay out the various registration attempts by both years and locations.

The first vital record registrations were attempted as soon as William Penn arrived in the state in 1682. Due to the differences in record-keeping in the colonial period of Pennsylvania from 1682 to 1789, I've focused on that period in a separate chapter, Chapter 8: Colonial Period Vital Records.

The main differences between registrations of births, marriages, and deaths and the later state-issued certificates are when the records were created relative to the event and what form the records had. While the certificates detailed in Chapters 3 and 4 were completed on individual forms with many people providing information, registrations were completed in ledger books by a single courthouse clerk. Doctors, midwives, funeral home directors, parents, and local registrars, all could be signing and providing information on certificates. On county registrations, it is often not known who provided the information to the clerk, and it could be recorded weeks to months after the event occurred.

Implementation of vital record registrations by counties and cities in Pennsylvania was directed by state law, which specifically defined what was to be collected, when, and by whom. (See Appendix B for detailed listing of the state laws related to vital records.) Later, when the Department of Health was formed in 1905, many of the rules around birth certificates and death certificates were dictated by policy boards and not widely published.

Most of the counties in the state followed a similar vital record registration process. The one exception was large industrial cities. The most populous city in the state, Philadelphia, followed different regulations than other locations. The key turning point in this differentiation was the Act of Consolidation on February 2, 1854 which turned the county border of Philadelphia into the new city border. Prior to consolidation, the City of Philadelphia was about one square mile in the middle of Philadelphia County. After consolidation, all the townships and boroughs in the county became part of the City and fell under its laws, and Philadelphia County no longer existed. Throughout this chapter, it will be noted where Philadelphia laws vary from the rest of the counties due to its unique status.

The other large industrial cities in Pennsylvania, such as Scranton, Reading, Allentown, and Pittsburgh, instituted Boards of Health in the latter half of the nineteenth century. These city departments issued birth and death registrations for their residents, while the rest of the county did not. For example, the City of Reading began vital record registrations in 1873, but the County of Berks which surrounds the City did not begin registrations until 1894. The dates of implementation varied by city and was controlled by state legislation.

Purpose of Vital Record Registrations

Birth and death registers attempted to collect vital statistics and track death rates from communicable diseases often found in cities. The Pennsylvania Assembly also required deaths be registered with the local Bureau of health for the following purposes:

- Obtain a burial permit for a local cemetery.
- Open probate proceedings for an estate.
- Remove an individual from the tax rolls.

Since all three of these purposes were essential for people to do, death registrations were done with close to full compliance.

Birth registrations did not have a purpose like death registrations did. There was nothing a child or parents needed it for. School was not mandatory in the nineteenth century, there was no driver's license, and Social Security was not invented yet. It would not be until the 1950s that birth records reached the compliance level of death records.

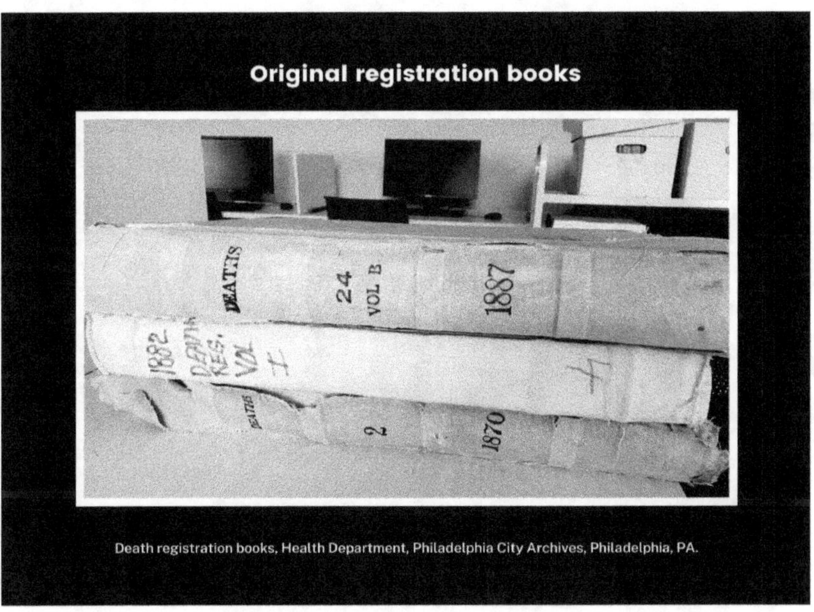

Death registration books, Health Department, Philadelphia City Archives, Philadelphia, PA.

County Registrations, 1852–1854

The first attempt at county registrations in the state occurred between 1852 and 1854. At that time, there were forty-eight counties in Pennsylvania, plus Philadelphia, which, as mentioned, incorporated its entire county into the city. These are the counties that did vital record registration during this time period:

Adams	Delaware	Montgomery
Allegheny	Elk	Montour
Armstrong	Franklin	Northampton
Beaver	Greene	Northumberland
Bedford	Huntingdon	Perry
Berks	Indiana	Schuylkill
Bradford	Juniata	Somerset
Bucks	Lancaster	Susquehanna
Butler	Lawrence	Tioga
Cambria	Lehigh	Union
Carbon	Luzerne	Venango
Centre	Lycoming	Warren
Chester	McKean	Washington
Columbia	Mercer	Wayne
Cumberland	Mifflin	Westmoreland
Dauphin	Monroe	York

State law required births, marriages, and deaths to be recorded at the Register of Wills at the local county courthouse. Compliance with registration during the period 1852 to 1854 was low. How low? It is unknown, but an examination of the surviving county records shows very few people registered their births, marriages, or deaths. No historian has provided a cause for the lack of participation from state residents. Regardless, the state law requiring registrations was repealed in 1855.

City Registrations, 1860–1915

As was mentioned, Pennsylvania's largest cities each had their own Department of Health or Bureau of Health. Each was required under state law to set up its own birth, marriage, and death registration systems. Researchers will find the forms and information collected for vital records varied from city to city, and over the years within each city.

The start date for birth and death registration depended on the size of the city. Philadelphia, Pennsylvania's largest city, went first with registrations in 1860. The next largest cities – Pittsburgh and Allentown – followed fourteen years later in 1874. Soon after that the state legislature required cities of ever decreasing size to comply with vital record registration. Here is chart of those dates:

Vital Record Registration in Cities

City	Start date by law
Philadelphia	July 1, 1860
Pittsburgh	May 1, 1870
Allentown	May 1, 1873
3rd class cities may enact (Erie, Harrisburg, Reading, Scranton)	May 5, 1874
Any city Board of Health may enact	May 5, 1876
3rd class cities must enact (Erie, Harrisburg, Reading, Scranton)	July 1, 1881
4th-7th class cities may enact	May 24, 1887

Individuals living within city borders registered with the city, and those outside the city were not required to register. Note that the same guidelines for recording births and deaths by location applied then like it applies now. If your ancestor traveled from his farm to the city, and suddenly died there, his death would be recorded in the city's death register.

There are dozens of varieties of birth, marriage, and death registrations since each locality created its own forms. Be prepared to examine each new form you encounter carefully. What was required to be on the forms by law is covered below.

Here is an example of a city registrations for births:

Birth registration in Philadelphia

Note: The doctor listed infants delivered for May and June on one form..

Birth registrations, Dr. Wm C. Todd, 1 May to 1 Jul 1868, Health Department, Philadelphia City Archives, Philadelphia, PA.

There was one odd error in the state legislation on city vital record registration during this period. When the state required the Department of Health in Harrisburg to begin issuing birth and death certificates in 1906, it forgot to stop the recording of birth and death registrations in Philadelphia until 1915. For eleven years there was dual recording of births and deaths in Philadelphia. Each person born, and each who died received a Philadelphia registration and a state-issued certificate. These were completed and filed in different ways and there may be differing information and name spellings between the two records. The city's registrations were microfilmed by FamilySearch and can be found on the website, and also in the City Archives.

County Registrations, 1893–1905

A second attempt at county vital record registration was more successful, but it still did not result in 100 percent compliance. From June 6, 1893 through December 31, 1905 each county's Orphans Court maintained two registers: one for deaths and one for births. Marriages were not a part of this legislation, because marriage license applications went into effect on October 1, 1885.

It is not known how complete these death and birth registrations are in each county. We can guess by the number of delayed birth certificates that were completed for people born during this time period that it was not 100 percent. The registrations collected by each county were compiled and sent to the Pennsylvania Bureau of Health.

Vital record registrations by counties and cities were short-lived. On April 27, 1905, the Pennsylvania State Legislature created the Department of Health and replaced county and city registrations with a uniform state-wide certificate system.

Information Collected on Local Registrations

In most locations, local registers of births, marriages, and deaths are large 18-inch by 24-inch ledger books, weighing several pounds each. There are multiple entries per page, either in columns going across or blocks of four on a page. The state defined the information to be collected, not the exact form for collection. This means researchers will find variations from county to county, county to city, and city to city.

Whether the vital record registration was conducted by city authorities or county ones, the types of information collected were similar.

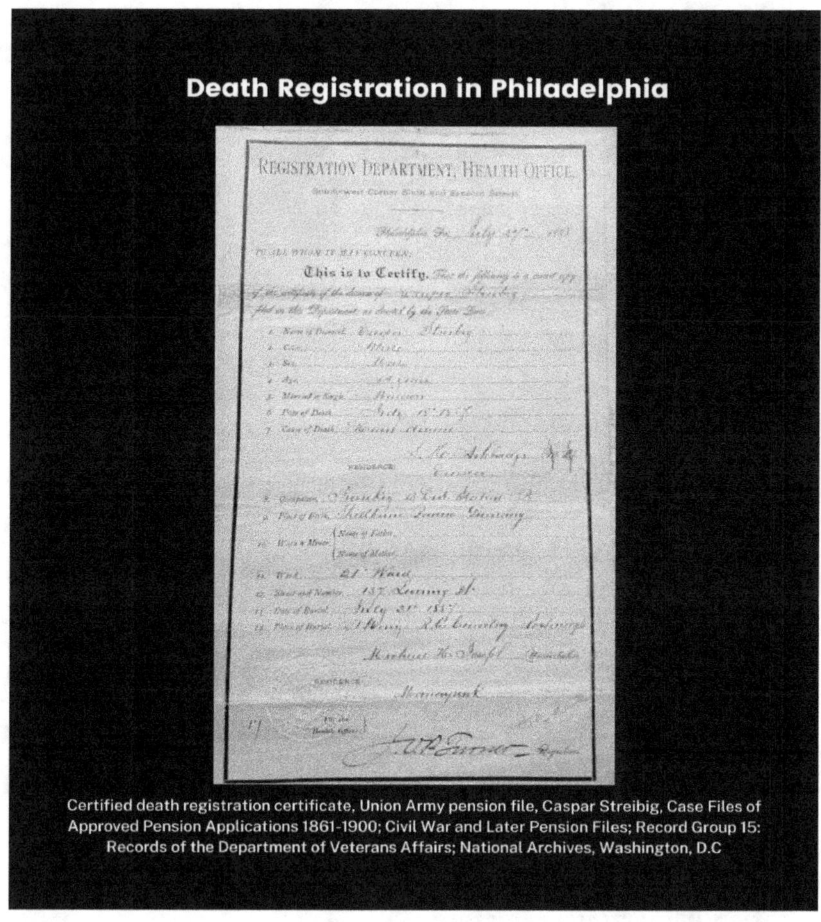

Certified death registration certificate, Union Army pension file, Caspar Streibig, Case Files of Approved Pension Applications 1861-1900; Civil War and Later Pension Files; Record Group 15: Records of the Department of Veterans Affairs; National Archives, Washington, D.C

Information in death registers

Generally, the following required information was noted:

- Full Name of Deceased
- Color/Race
- Sex
- Date of Death
- Age at Death

- Married or Single
- Residence
- Length of Time at Residence
- Occupation
- Cause of Death
- Onset/Length (of illness)
- Parents' Names if Minor
- Parents' Birthplace
- Physician Name/Signature, Address and Date
- Undertaker Name, Address and Date
- Burial Place/Cemetery
- Date of Burial
- Registrar Name and Date

Information in marriage registers

These registers were maintained prior to marriage licenses which began in 1885. Generally, the following required information was noted:

- Full Names of Bride and Groom
- Color/Race
- Sex
- Age
- Previously Married?
- Residence

- Length of Time at Residence
- Occupation
- Parents' Names if Minor
- Parents' Birthplace
- Date of Marriage
- Registrar Name and Date

Information in birth registers

Generally, the following required information was noted:

- Full Name of Child
- Color/Race
- Sex
- Date of Birth
- Residence
- Parents' Names
- Parents' Birthplace
- Physician Name/Signature, Address and Date
- Registrar Name and Date

Process to Complete Local Registrations

The county and city registration process for deaths and births usually started with physicians. State law compelled physicians to report on the deaths of those in their care. In the nineteenth through mid-twentieth centuries, doctors made home visits for those at the end of life. The doctor would record the last time he saw the patient alive and estimate time of death. Hospital use was uncommon in cities and non-existent in rural areas, so the actual witnessing of a death by a doctor or nurse was rare. For birth registrations, midwives in addition to doctors, were required to submit information. Not every birth was attended by a licensed medical provider, and those births attended at home by family members likely went un-registered.

Vital record registration was completed in-person at the county courthouse at the Register of Wills, Orphans Court, or Health Department office, depending on the year and location. Researchers will notice in rural county death registration records that physicians sometimes reported two or more deaths or births occurring weeks apart in one courthouse visit. Timeliness was required, but not always followed, in less-populated areas.

Tax assessors also assisted in the compliance with death registrations and birth registrations. In the nineteenth century, tax assessors were assigned to each municipality – township, borough, or city – and would go door-to-door to collect what was due each spring and fall. Taxes were paid to the county by heads of households and men over age twenty one. If the tax collector came to a property and found that some of the taxable residents had died, he would report the death to the Register of Wills office and sometimes mark the resident as "deceased" in his tax roll. Likewise, if he found the household had children born since his last visit, he would note the information to be recorded in the birth ledger books. If you examine the birth registrations in a county from 1893 to 1905, you will find dozens of children or more listed each May and December, no matter when the birth occurred.

Wives, single women, and children did not pay county taxes and were not listed on local tax rolls. Because of this, when women and children died in the nineteenth century, their deaths were not always reported. The exception here, of course, was women who were heads of households and responsible for taxes, particularly in rural areas, where up to 20 percent of properties in a township could be headed by women. Those women could be on the tax rolls and when they died, listed on the death register.

How to Find Vital Record Registrations

The Register of Wills at the county courthouse typically kept birth, death, and marriage registrations. In some counties, the records will be found at the Orphans' Court office. In cities, records were maintained by the local Department of Health or Bureau of Health, but most of these, except Philadelphia's, were abolished in 1905 when the state Department of Health was formed. Regardless of where the records were created over a hundred years ago, they are now preserved in local archives, courthouses, and on FamilySearch and Ancestry.

The FamilySearch Catalog is the recommended starting point for these local registrations. As of June 2024, most of these records do not show up in search results, but the digital images are there. In the Catalog view, type in "Pennsylvania, [County Name]" (where County Name is the county you want) to search what county records are available. If you want to search a city, then add it after the county (Only the largest cities have their own category in the catalog.).

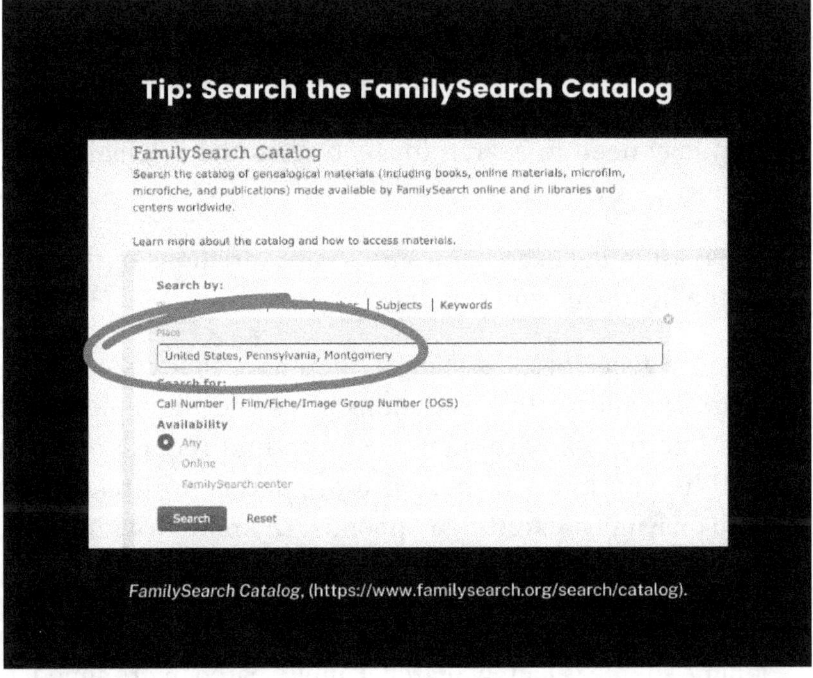

FamilySearch Catalog, (https://www.familysearch.org/search/catalog).

The one exception is the smallest vital record registration collection. The few county vital records between 1852 and 1854 that survive are digitized on Ancestry in these three databases:

- Pennsylvania, U.S., Births, 1852-1854": **https://www.ancestry.com/search/collections/2349/**
- "Pennsylvania, U.S., Deaths, 1852-1854": **https://www.ancestry.com/search/collections/2487/**
- "Pennsylvania, U.S., Marriages, 1852-1854": **https://www.ancestry.com/search/collections/2486/**

Checklist for Searching

- First, know the county the person died in. If unsure, look at the cemetery record and last census record for the county of residence and start there.
- Be aware of the historical county boundaries for your ancestor. Between 1682 and 1878, new counties were created, and county lines were frequently redrawn. When tracing your ancestral line, you may need to search for records in the original or parent county.
- To assist in the search, be sure to use variations of the spelling of the first name and surname.
- County genealogical societies often have indexes of the birth, marriage, and death registrations. These were completed before the internet and are often useful to find records. The index will let you know if there is a original record to request or find on FamilySearch. See Appendix D: Archives with Historical Records for a list of local societies.
- For city and county birth and death registrations, the primary online source is FamilySearch. FamilySearch microfilmed many

historical courthouse records in the mid-to-late twentieth century. Since most of these records were in ledger books, there is usually an index in the front of each book. Check the beginning of each microfilm collection for that index to find your ancestor, then go through the images to get to correct page. Original records are most likely still at county courthouses. See Appendix C: Sources for Vital Records for a list of county courthouses.

- Be sure to collect the registrations for all related family members of the deceased. Analyzing these will provide details to the life of your direct line ancestor.

Book Bonus: To help you in your vital records research, I have created a free research plan template you can download. Go to **https://www.paancestors.com/book-bonuses/**to get it.

Chapter 6

Marriage License Applications

History of Marriage Licenses

MARRIAGE HAS EXISTED FOR all of human history. In European history, the church had jurisdiction over who could marry and maintained records of their members' marriages. It wasn't until the Marriage Act of 1836 that the British government recognized marriage with no need for a minister's blessing. Yet these marriages – and all marriages of other religious faiths – were recorded with the Church of England, the official religion of Britain. A marriage was not recognized as a legal marriage no matter who conducted it, unless it was in the registers of the Church.

From the start of Pennsylvania, things were different. Pennsylvania was a province, not a colony of England at first, and as such set it own laws. One of the first laws in Pennsylvania allowed for religious freedom, and soon more than two dozen faiths were present. Each religious faith had its own traditions and requirements for marriage. If someone did not like the rules under one religion, he or she could switch to a different one. There was no central church register of marriages.

However, Pennsylvania's founder, William Penn, followed the English tradition and mandated the registration of marriages to begin in 1682. Again in 1701 and 1730, the Province put requirements on marriages (See Appendix B: Selected Pennsylvania Laws Relating to Vital Records). Unfortunately, surviving records show that few marriages were recorded. One explanation for the lack of compliance with the law is that registration of marriage with the local courthouse was not something people did prior to arrival in the province (England had no such law for another 140 years.). Or perhaps people viewed registration as unnecessary since any marriage performed by a religious leader was legal in terms of inheritance and property ownership. Registration did not make a marriage legal, the ceremony before a priest, minister, or rabbi did in Pennsylvania.

Another attempt at marriage registrations by the Pennsylvania government occurred between 1852 and 1854. It required newly married couples to record their marriage after the fact with the Register of Wills at their local county courthouse. Similar to 150 years prior, few marriages were registered. These marriages in the records appear to be the wealthiest residents of the county. Perhaps those residents were closest to the courthouse or had reliable transportation for the journey.

The lack of marriage registrations during these various leglislative attempts, might lead one to think that couple were cohabitating and not getting married at all. An examination of religious records during the first 200 years of Pennsylvania history would refute this idea. Priests, ministers, and rabbis were marrying tens of thousands of couples every year. These were recorded in each local church or synagogue ledger book. The certificate they received from the wedding ceremony was considered a legal document. It was all that was needed to prove inheritance of an estate upon the death of a spouse.

By 1885, Pennsylvania determined it needed have formal, uniform records of marriages in the state. Pennsylvania residents would still be married by their religious leaders or government officials, but the state required their approval first in the form of a marriage license. The marriage license acted as a permit to get married and without one, a couple was not considered legally married. This law came with significant fines for clergy and other officiants who married couples without marriage licenses.

There is an exception to the law requiring a marriage license: common law marriage. A common law marriage is one in which a man and women cohabitate and declare to each other they are husband and wife. Pennsylvania recognized common law marriage from its founding in 1682. Common law marriage was abolished in Pennsylvania in 2004, effective January 1, 2005.

Regulations for Marriage Licenses

The Pennsylvania regulation of marriages through marriage license applications sought to ensure specific rules were enforced. State laws specified who could get married based on four criteria:

1. Current marital status
2. Consanguinity
3. Age
4. Gender

1.Current Marital Status

The biggest prohibition in marriage is having more than one spouse at a time. This is known as bigamy or polygamy if more than two spouses. By law, a person can be married to only one other person at a time. If an individual was married to more than one person, most courts recognize the first marriage and not the second (or subsequent) marriage. The law in Pennsylvania has always allowed for only one marriage partner at a time.

2. Consanguinity

The second concern of the state is consanguinity, or couples too closely related biologically. In Pennsylvania, an individual cannot marry his or her parent, grandparent, child, grandchild, sibling, aunt, uncle, niece, nephew, or first cousin. This law has been consistent over state history. Some question "Why would a grandparent and grandchild marry?" and the answer is "Inheritance." There have been cases of a grandparent marrying a grandchild, not for sexual relations, but for the ability to pass inheritance directly to the grandchild, and pass over his or her own child. Laws of inheritance pass estates first to the spouse, then children, so such a marriage would skip over a generation would prevent children from inheriting what was legally theirs.

3. Age

The third concern in marriage is that each person be of adult age. The age of adulthood varied over state history. Since 1972, both partners are required to be eighteen or older to be married as adults. Individuals aged between sixteen and eighteen years old can get married with parent or guardian permission. Prior to 1972, to be married as an adult required the bride and groom to be age twenty-one. Those under twenty-one years old and at least sixteen years old required parent or guardian permission. The minimum age of marriage was set at sixteen years old in 1872. For a short time from June 1871 to 1872, the minimum age for marriage was set at twenty-one years old. Prior to June 1871 there was no state law stating a minimum age, because marriage rules were dictated by religious leaders, not the government.

4. Gender

Pennsylvania marriage law did not specify gender, other than the term 'bride' and 'groom' on marriage license applications until 1996. The Defense of Marriage Act of 1996 limited marriage to male and female in the state. This law effectively banned same-sex marriage. The 1996 law was overturned by federal courts on May 20, 2014 and current state law does not specify gender at all on the marriage license application.

Once a couple has met all the requirements outlined above, they can proceed with completing an application for a marriage license in one of Pennsylvania's counties. Most couples apply in the county where they live. Some apply in the county where the marriage will take place. And still others will cross state lines for their marriage, which means the couple's marriage license in that state's records, not Pennsylvania's, even though the couple lives in Pennsylvania.

Pennsylvania, like all states, recognizes marriages made in any state under that state's laws. For some couples, marrying in another state was done because they could not or would not comply with their own state's laws.

Marriage License Application Process

The marriage license process requires three steps: the marriage license application, the ceremony, and the return of duplicate certificate.

Top half of marriage license application

Marriage license application, Horace Wilmer and Sarah Helman, no, 12632, 9 Dec 1902, microfilm, Montgomery County Archives, Eagleville, PA.

Detailed steps to apply for a license

Here is the process of the marriage license in detail:

Step 1: Marriage license application is completed.

- The bride and groom appear at the courthouse together to complete the marriage license application. Typically, this is no more than a week prior to the marriage. It can be as much as a month, or the same day as the marriage.
- The clerk from the Register of Wills office or Orphans' Court office authorizes the marriage to be performed.
- A fee is paid at the time of the marriage license application.

Step 2: The marriage ceremony is performed.

- The marriage ceremony is conducted by an officiant. This could be clergy, or a civil servant such as a judge or courthouse official.
- The officiant completes the duplicate certificate stating he or she conducted the marriage at a specific date and place.

Step 3: The duplicate certificate is returned.

- The officiant signs and returns the duplicate certificate to the Register of Wills office or Orphans' Court office.
- Once the duplicate certificate is received, the clerk issues an official marriage certificate with a raised seal to the couple. No copy of this certificate is maintained in the office.
- This official marriage certificate is typically mailed to the couple's home.

Bottom half of marriage license application

Note: Duplicate certificate signed by minister confirming marriage completed.

DUPLICATE CERTIFICATE.

Duplicate Certificate of Marriage.

Marriage license application, Horace Wilmer and Sarah Helman, no, 12632, 9 Dec 1902, microfilm, Montgomery County Archives, Eagleville, PA.

<u>A marriage is not valid (legal) unless all three steps are completed.</u>

Observant genealogists will note that it is possible for a couple to apply for a marriage license and not complete the marriage ceremony. The verification that a marriage ceremony was performed is indicated by the return of the duplicate certificate to the courthouse. In most cases, clerks would make a notation on the marriage license application that the certificate was returned or if the marriage did not occur. If there is no notation of the duplicate certificate being returned, its possible the marriage did not happen. Check the adjoining marriage license applications of other couples to see what the normal recording process was for those clerks at that time. The most difficult thing to prove is something that did not happen (we only have information on events that do happen), so genealogists should take note to assemble additional documentation from newspapers, wills, pensions, and death certificates to confirm the marriage.

About common law marriage

A common law marriage in Pennsylvania is when a man and woman, without a legal marriage recognized by the state, reside together and refer to each other as husband and wife in public. In the past, Pennsylvania upheld common law marriages through individual court cases brought to the Court of Common Pleas. On November 24, 2004 the state legislature passed Pennsylvania Consolidated Statue § 1103, and declared all common law marriages on and after January 2, 2005 to be invalid. All common law marriages occurring prior to the law passage are still considered valid and evidence of those will still appear in county civil court records.

County civil court records are where common law marriages are found. A court filing was required because one of the spouses had died and property needed to be passed to the surviving common law spouse. There may also be evidence in probate (estate) records and census records where a spouse is named. So, if a marriage license cannot be located in any county or state for a marriage in 2004 or earlier, it is possible the couple did a common law marriage and county court records should be consulted.

Information Collected on Marriage License Applications

Marriage licenses typically contain the following information for each person:

- Name
- Residence
- Age
- Race
- Parents' names and residence

- Occupation
- Attestation that one is not already married
- Parental permission, if necessary

At various times in the twentieth-century, Pennsylvania placed additional requirements on adults wanting to marry. These included:

- Having no communicable diseases as proven in a blood test
- Being mentally competent and not under the influence of drugs or alcohol, no mental illness, no mental incapacity
- Able to financially support a wife and children (question for men only)
- No physical disability
- Follow at least a three-day waiting period between marriage license application and the marriage ceremony

How to Find Marriage License Applications

Marriage license applications are a county-created record and the original applications are preserved in the courthouse where the application was made. Pennsylvania's Department of Health only collects basic information from the counties, such as names and dates. to compile vital statistics on number of marriages. Genealogists wanting the full marriage record with all the information listed above need to contact the county courthouse.

Marriage licenses began uniformly in every county Orphans' Court in 1885. Cities were the exception to this law and began doing marriage registrations (post marriage records) as early as 1860. On January 1, 1886, Philadelphia followed what all the other counties in Pennsylvania were doing. In 1915, Philadelphia moved its marriage license application from the Orphans' Court to a Marriage License Bureau. The city still followed state law and used the same application form and process.

These marriage documents are considered a public record from the moment they are created. A researcher could walk into any Pennsylvania courthouse and ask to see the list of who applied to be married that day, or yesterday, or anytime in the past. Anyone can look up a marriage license issued for anyone at any time. Unlike state-issued birth certificates and death certificates, you do not need to prove you are related to the people on the record. This openness of marriage records helps prevent bigamy in the state's view.

Historically, marriage licenses in each county were assigned a number, beginning on January 1 of each year. The numbering continued upward by one with each marriage license application filed. At the end of the year, the applications were bound into ledger books and labeled "Marriage License Docket," by calendar year. In less populous, rural counties, marriage license docket books extend over a few years. Because the licenses are arranged in chronological order by date of application, each ledger book is indexed by surname of the bride and groom (now partner one and partner two).

The final part of the marriage license application is the duplicate certificate. Duplicate certificates are filed in one of three ways: with the original marriage license application; under "Marriage License Returns"; or under a separate ledger book entitled, "Duplicate Marriage Certificates." If parental or guardian consent was needed, this is usually noted on the marriage license or on a separate paper and filed with the application.

Most counties have put older marriage records into archival storage, offsite from the current office in the courthouse. Additionally, some counties have microfilmed or microfiched older marriage license applications to save storage space. Some marriage license applications were microfilmed by FamilySearch, but these are not universally searchable from the main search box. The majority of these documents are in the FamilySearch Catalog of digitized and not yet indexed records. If doing an in-person research trip to the courthouse, contact the courthouse by phone or email to confirm the location of records before you go.

Checklist for Searching

Steps to locate marriage license applications:

- Estimate the marriage date. You will want to narrow down the likely year of the marriage before beginning a search. One way to determine the year of marriage is the U.S. census. From 1900 to 1950 the census asked married couples how many years they were married. Prior to 1900, a way to calculate the marriage year is based from the birth of the first child. It was common then to marry anytime from six months to three years prior to the birth of the first child.

- Know the county to focus on for your search. Again, the census closest to the estimated marriage date is likely the county of marriage for the couple. Also check adjoining counties. Some couples married in adjoining states. For example, Maryland waived blood tests prior to marriage and so was a popular destination for couples in the 1960s.

- Check the indexed marriage records. Both Ancestry and FamilySearch have databases of indexed and searchable marriage records. Currently the Ancestry database of marriages is just names and dates, and appears to be loaned from FamilySearch, with the images of the original records still on FamilySearch. One example of such a database from Ancestry is "Pennsylvania Marriages 1852–1968" **https://www.ancestry.com/search/collections/61381**. Unfortunately, this easy-to-use database is only a small percentage of all the marriage licenses issued in the state, so do not despair if an ancestor is not there.

- Check the unindexed digital images. Billions of records on FamilySearch are not yet indexed for computer searching. To access these records for Pennsylvania, go to familysearch.org and then choose the Catalog. Type in "Pennsylvania, [County Name]" to see the list of available record types for the county you are searching. Scroll down to the category "Vital Records" to see the available marriage records.

FamilySearch Catalog, (https://www.familysearch.org/search/catalog).

- Contact the county courthouse. Once online possibilities have been exhausted, it is time for old-school genealogy work. The originals of all marriage records for any county in Pennsylvania are available at the county courthouse or the archive the county uses. For example, in Philadelphia, the City Hall: Marriage Licenses Department, is the contact for copies: **https://www.phila.gov/services/birth-marriage-life-events/marriage-and-divorce/find-and-request-a-marriage-record/**. In Pittsburgh, the City County Building: Marriage Department, holds all the marriage license applications not just for the city but for all of Allegheny County: **https://www.alleghenycounty.us/Government/Records/Marriage-Records**. See Appendix C: Government Sources for Vital Records for a listing of every county courthouse and their archive.

- For marriage records prior to 1885, use substitutes such as religious records, newspapers, military pension records (a wife would be listed along with date of marriage and proof from the minister or justice of the peace), family Bibles, and census records.

Book Bonus: To help you in your vital records research, I have created a free research plan template you can download. Go to **https://www.paancestors.com/book-bonuses/**to get it.

Chapter 7

Divorce Decrees

History of Divorce in Pennsylvania

DIVORCE IS THE DISSOLUTION of a marriage through a decree by a government official. Pennsylvania since its founding has always had a legal process for divorce. This was unusual among the American colonies. Most of Pennsylvania's founding laws followed English Common Law, and England provided no mechanism for married couples to divorce until 1857.

The initial law in the Province of Pennsylvania gave authority only to the Proprietor (governor) to dissolve marriages. The legal reasons he could dissolve a marriage included incest, homosexuality, adultery, or bigamy by one of partners in the marriage. The governor appears to have used his authority in only a few cases. Within the minutes of the meetings of the Provincial Council there is mention of requests for divorce, including the colorful details of the circumstances.[1]

In 1785, nine years after the first state constitution, a divorce law was passed by the Assembly. It was the first law in the new nation to allow cruelty as a reason for divorce. The other reasons covered in this law, in addition to the existing reasons mentioned above, included inability to procreate and desertion. The authority to grant divorce was given to two governmental entities at that time: the Supreme Court of Pennsylvania and the state legislature.

In 1854, the power to grant divorce was transferred to each county's Court of Common Pleas. The Pennsylvania Legislature and Pennsylvania Supreme Court still retained their powers of divorce, but they ruled in only the most serious or consequential divorce cases. County Prothonotaries began keeping separate divorce dockets in 1878 (Prior to 1878, divorce cases are listed in the Appearance Docket.). By 1895 state authorities removed themselves, and counties were processing all divorces, with local judges issuing divorce decrees. Pennsylvania continues with this same process today.

During this entire history of divorce so far, divorce was only granted if one partner could prove in court that the other partner was at fault. In other words, a crime – adultery, bigamy, desertion, incest, cruelty, infertility, or homosexuality – had to have been committed for the marriage to be dissolved. Witnesses were used to prove fault, and testimony was sworn under oath. Researchers reading divorce proceedings will often find emotional and brutal descriptions of a couple's relationship issues.

Today we have "no fault divorce." No-fault divorce began in April 1980 and allows for a couple to dissolve their marriage by mutual agreement. No cause is required. One partner usually still initiates the divorce case in the courts, but it is common today to have both spouses agree to dissolve the marriage in a more peaceful manner than historically was the case.

Divorce Process

All divorce cases are listed on court dockets by a plaintiff and a defendant. The plaintiff is the spouse who initiates the divorce. The defendant is the spouse who responds to the accusations of the other. Prior to 1980, the plaintiff spouse would detail the accusations against his or her partner. He or she would need to provide enough evidence, that his or her spouse committed one of the following:

- Bigamy – currently married to another person at the same time

- Cruelty – abuse of a married partner
- Desertion – no contact or financial support for six months or longer
- Inability to procreate – the man or woman is unable to conceive and carry a child to term
- Incest – marriage between two adults who are closely related (consanguinity)
- Homosexuality – one of the partners is attracted to the same sex
- Adultery – one of the partners is in a sexual relationship outside of the marriage
- Felony Conviction – one of the partners committed a serious crime
- Lunacy – only applied to women, and if the wife was declared a lunatic, she was eligible to be divorced
- Habitual drunkenness – usually applied to men, and made husband eligible for divorce

In order to prove one of the above crimes, testimony was given before a judge. Divorce court cases are commonly full of graphic descriptions, sometimes including physical and emotional violence. Researchers may find evidence of divorce in a newspaper search. Details often made their way into local newspapers, because divorce hearings took place in courts open to the public. Family historians should be aware that what they find out may cause emotional distress. Consider having a disinterested person read divorce files first on your behalf.

Married couples with children had additional concerns. Children from a divorced marriage could be declared illegitimate, in other words, having no father. For example, state law allowed a husband divorcing his wife to claim that child(ren) of the marriage were not his natural (biological) child(ren). This claim, if proved in court, meant he did not have to financially support the child(ren). Additionally in Pennsylvania law, children automatically inherit the estates of their parents upon their death. If a husband declared child(ren) from marriage illegitimate, then this inheritance law did not apply. It was not until the 1970s that state law defined the rights of all children – biological, adopted, and step children – equal before the law, and financial support from each parent was given to them.

Divorce proceedings usually took several months to move through the court. A single judge, not a jury, presided over the case and issued the divorce decree (or not). A judge could grant one of two types of divorce: a complete dissolution of the marriage vows, or a legal separation, also called a "bed and board divorce." A complete dissolution in the form of a divorce decree was the most common and allowed each partner to marry again. A legal separation allowed the woman to retain her dower rights (rights to some of her husband's estate after his death) and access to some form of alimony, or financial support.

Annulment and church law

The term "annulment" has different meanings in civil law and church law (or canon law). In church law, annulment is the dissolution of a marriage as if it never existed. Record of the marriage in church records is removed. This is beyond annulment in civil law, which dissolves the marriage, but still recognizes the fact the marriage occurred. The government's record of the marriage, most of the time a marriage license application, is not destroyed when a divorce or annulment is granted. Governments annul marriages that violate one of the four conditions listed at the beginning of this chapter.

However, church leaders could determine that a marriage was invalid from the minute it was performed. Churches annulled marriages for the following reasons: bigamy, consanguinity, and impotence on the part of the husband. Historically, when a church annulled a marriage, no divorce decree was issued. Today with our many-layered bureaucratic systems, couples who get an annulment also get a divorce decree so there is no question of their marital status.

Information Collected During Divorce Proceedings

In the earliest divorce records conducted by state officials, minimal information is found. A few lines in legislative records or court records would list only the names of the parties involved, the date, the reason for the divorce, and the judge's or state legislature's ruling in the divorce request. Further details of what occurred in the couple's relationship are not in these official records. However, a persistent researcher may look for letters to Pennsylvania state office holders from their constituents requesting a divorce. These personal letters would be found in the archives of the Pennsylvania House in Harrisburg.

When divorce authority was transferred to the counties, more information was recorded. Divorce went through civil court and was often contentious. In a divorce file, one may find the following:

- Petition to the court, stating the names of people involved and reason for divorce
- Depositions of witnesses
- Court proceedings
- Subpoenas of witnesses
- Interrogatories, also known as Discovery
- Answer Petition, from Respondent (Defendant) often denying charges against him/her
- Divorce Decree from the Judge
- Petition for Payment, usually from the wife to the husband

In the days before television shows, these divorce cases before the county judge must have drawn quite a bit of interest in the community.

How to Find Divorce Records

There is some overlap and confusion as divorce moved from the state level to the county level. If researching in the period between 1854 and 1895, check both state-level records and county-level records.

For divorces prior to 1881, the Pennsylvania Supreme Court or state legislature (also known as the General Assembly) would be the record holder. The annual compiled legislative book, *Laws of Pennsylvania*, notes divorces granted by the General Assembly. Copies of these books are found in law libraries. The records of the state Supreme Court are kept at the Pennsylvania State Archive in Harrisburg.

Divorce proceedings after 1854 could have begun in the county court where the couple resided. Between 1854 and 1881, records may be found in either the county or the state legislature records. To search county records, contact the Prothonotary office. Divorces are in the Appearance Docket until 1878 and then the Divorce Docket from 1878 to today. These Docket books are typically kept by calendar quarter, or by court of legislative session. It is common for the books to be indexed by plaintiff and defendant, so check under both indexes for the husband and wife.

The docket usually only lists the names, dates, reason for divorce, and if granted. Genealogists should request the entire divorce file from the Prothonotary to obtain all the documentation related to the divorce.

Checklist for Searching

- First, confirm that the couple was legally married in Pennsylvania or another state.
- Next, confirm that the couple was living in Pennsylvania at the time of the divorce. Pennsylvania did not divorce non-residents for most of its history. To be divorced in Pennsylvania courts means that the couple resided in Pennsylvania. Tax records, local directories, land deeds, and census records will confirm a

location for the couple.

- Check the Prothonotary in the county of residence at the time of the divorce. Even if it was before the time the office formally recorded divorces, this county office would be a good place to start.

- After the 1980 Divorce Law, Pennsylvania couples could file their divorces in any county, not just the county they lived in. Densely population counties would have judges' dockets fill up quickly, so couples could be waiting six months or longer to begin divorce proceedings. To speed up the process, they had the option to file in another Pennsylvania county which had no wait time on the dockets.

- In the years when only the state could grant divorce, the Pennsylvania Supreme Court records are the place to start. These are located at the Pennsylvania State Archives. Some have been microfilmed. You need to know the possible year(s) of the divorce before contacting them.

- The Assembly could also grant divorces until 1874. These state legislature records are difficult to locate. Genealogists should check for the private laws (laws passed for individuals) in the Sessions Laws and Pamphlet Laws. Currently portions of the state laws are digitized online at **https://www.palrb.us**. To search other years, contact a local law library in Pennsylvania. Candy Crocker Livengood's book, *Genealogical Abstracts of the Laws of Pennsylvania and the Statues at Large,* abstracts divorces as well as other personal events up to 1810.

---

1. Meehan, Thomas R., "'Not Made Out of Levity' Evolution of Divorce in Early Pennsylvania," *Pennsylvania Magazine of History and Biography*, October 1933 (https://journals.psu.edu/pmhb/article/view/42441).

Chapter 8

Colonial Period Vital Records

DURING THE COLONIAL PERIOD, Pennsylvania was formally known as the Province of Pennsylvania. Pennsylvania was not technically founded as a colony of the English Crown, unlike other American colonies. The founder, William Penn, established his Province with a charter, essentially a property deed, on March 4, 1681. Pennsylvania considers this date its founding date. In 1682, the Province's first laws went into effect and and most historical records date to this year.

Penn started Pennsylvania using many traditions of his homeland, England. One tradition he carried over was the Church of England's practice of creating local registers of births, marriages, and deaths. Pennsylvania did not have a government-imposed religion, so Penn put vital record registration under control of his county administrators.

It seems that very few of Pennsylvania's first residents complied with the requirement to register births, marriages, and deaths. Or perhaps many did comply, but those records no longer exist. One unfortunate practice over the years between 1682 and today was that as records were transcribed or microfilmed, original records were tossed in the rubbish. Sometimes records were even disposed of without any preservation of their information, if they were records of what were considered insignificant people of the time (enslaved, indentured, landless, etc). It is now Pennsylvania law that no historical records can be disposed of without informing the State Archives first. Sadly, there was much record loss over the past three hundred plus years.

The Pennsylvania Archives Books

What records we have of early Pennsylvania survive today in *The Pennsylvania Archives* book series. *The Pennsylvania Archives* were published in nine different series, with 138 volumes across the series. For researchers focused on colonial-era vital records, marriage records are found in the following volumes:

- Marriages prior to 1810: *2nd Series, Volumes I, II, VIII, and IX*
- Marriage licenses, 1784-1786: *6th Series, Volume VI,* p. 285-310
- Marriage licenses prior to 1790: *2nd Series, Volume* II
- Marriages recorded by the Registrar General, 1685-1689: *2nd Series, Volume VIII*

Neither birth or death registrations are in the *Pennsylvania Archives* books. However, family historians will find church baptisms, cemetery listings, and military records which can act as vital record substitutes. *The Guide to the Published Archives of Pennsylvania* by Henry Howard Eddy, published by the Pennsylvania Historical and Museum Commission in 1949, provides an overview and organization to collections in the series.

All of *The Pennsylvania Archives* series have been digitized and made available to search for free on Ancestry and Fold3. They can also be found in the FamilySearch online library, Internet Archive, and HathiTrust. The simplest way to search for an ancestor in one of these books is to pull up a digital copy and search by that ancestor's surname.

If the name of this book series is confusing to you because it is named after the institution, the Pennsylvania Archives, you are not alone. Many researchers have been befuddled by references to "The Pennsylvania Archives", not knowing if it referred to the books or the building.

Private Law Legislation and Governor's Orders

Citizens of the province were able to petition the provincial council and governor for assistance in personal matters. Within the ten published volumes of the *Minutes of the Provincial Council* are instances of these petitions and their resolution. The legislature would listen to the complaint and request for relief, then pass a law just for those individuals involved, declaring a resolution. These types of laws are called private laws and occurred in Pennsylvania until 1874 when the new state constitution outlawed them. Its possible your ancestor had a private law passed on his or her behalf.

Researchers can find these private laws passed during the colonial period within the *Minutes of the Provincial Council.* Digital copies are on Internet Archive and Google Books. An easy to click through list of all the volumes (including *The Pennsylvania Archives* books above) is on Wikipedia in the "Pennsylvania Archives" article here: **https://en.wikipedia.org/wiki/Pennsylvania_Archives**. Each digital copy can be searched for surnames of interest.

Pay Attention to County Names and Boundaries

Understanding the historical changes in Pennsylvania's county boundaries is necessary for colonial era research.

Pennsylvania was originally founded with just three counties in 1682. By 1776, this number had grown to eleven counties, covering an area that was only two-thirds the size of the present state. Following the end of the Revolutionary War and the adoption of the state constitution in 1790, Pennsylvania expanded to twenty-one counties and began to take on much of its current shape. These changes continued over time, with new counties being added and boundaries redrawn until 1878. When researching your ancestors, keep these historical shifts in mind, as you may need to look for records in different counties based on the time period you are researching. See Appendix E: Additional Resources for Research for two reliable maps for historical county boundaries.

There are many decades between the founding of Pennsylvania and the first state-wide efforts at vital records in late nineteenth century. For those seeking evidence of births, marriages, and deaths in this gap (and any time really!), consult the list of Substitutes for Vital Records in Chapter 10.

Chapter 9

Unexpected and Unknown Parentage

ONE COULD SAY THAT the focus of most genealogical work involves unknown or unexpected parentage. Researchers spend much of their time finding the parents of an ancestor so they can climb further up the family tree.

However, this chapter covers situations where the ancestor was conceived outside of marriage, orphaned as a child, and/or adopted. Many of these situations arise in genealogical work. These are also the most difficult problems to resolve, because the documentation to prove the biological parent of a child was either never created, not preserved, or remains sealed in government files.

This chapter will cover three common circumstances of unexpected or unknown parentage:

- Children born outside of marriage, formerly called illegitimacy
- Death of one or both parents, commonly called orphan children
- Change in parental-child relationship, also known as adoption

The records historically created for children and parents around these events is described below, along with a suggested approach for research. Details provided are on the laws and customs of Pennsylvania only, so if research crosses to another state, the laws and customs of that state would apply. Where DNA testing can help, a brief description is given of what it can provide. It is beyond the scope of this book to provide detailed directions of how to use DNA to identify unexpected or unknown parents. For more resources on that topic, see Appendix E: Additional Resources for Research.

Illegitimacy

A child born outside of a legal marriage was labeled as illegitimate under state law. Illegitimacy is a legal term, but it has also been used to make people feel uncomfortable and ashamed. It replaced the even more shameful term "bastard" used in legal documents prior to about 1880. Neither term is used to described children today, but a genealogist must know these historical terms to research effectively.

There are no statistics to tell us how many children were conceived outside of marriage over the decades. People presume a child born in marriage is biologically the child of the wife and husband. Now because of DNA results on genealogy websites, many people see that their ancestors had children outside of marriage.

What is the DNA evidence that tells a researcher there was an illegitimate child? In autosomal DNA test results (the most common DNA test taken), the test taker will find parent(s), cousins, and siblings with whom they share DNA but are not documented in the existing records. These "new" parent(s), cousins and siblings are the other DNA test takers who happened to have also tested on the same genealogy website. There may always be other relatives out there not yet known.

What a genealogist chooses to do with this information is a personal choice. Some genealogists trace both the genetic family tree and the existing documented family tree, and share both. Other genealogists simply make a note on the record of the child of the biological parent and leave the child with the documented parents who raised him or her. It is a situation each person navigates the best they can. It is outside the scope of this book (and worth an entire book itself!) to detail the process of DNA analysis and suggested ways to approach unexpected biological family. For additional resources, see Appendix E for suggested resources.

Historical laws on illegitimacy

For researchers working on building out a family tree with known or suspected illegitimately conceived ancestors, some knowledge of historical illegitimacy law is helpful. For about half of Pennsylvania history, an illegitimate child was considered *filius nullius* (nobody's child) and had no right to inherit property from either the father or mother. A child in this circumstance could have been left at an orphanage or could have been raised by other family members, taking their surname (informal adoption). Many times, the child took the surname of the mother and lived with the mother if she could financially support him or her. The father was expected to pay some amount of money weekly or monthly until the child was about eight years old. At that age, it was felt that the child could begin working and supporting himself or herself. The local county administrated this payment from the father to the mother which was called a "bastardy bond."

The bastardy bond was imposed on the father after trial before the Court of Quarter Sessions, criminal court. These bonds did not have their own set of books or indexes like adoption and divorce proceedings did; they were a part of the regular court proceedings. In the Appearance Docket books by court term, researchers will first find the name of the pregnant unmarried woman. She was usually called in first to state who the father of the child was. If she did not tell, the bond was posted to her parents to support the child. Most women gave the name of the father, and he was then called into court. The father's name will also be in the Appearance Docket, in this second court appearance for the bastardy bond. Sometimes there is just one appearance of the usually pregnant mother and the father together. Also listed in these cases are two to three witnesses to give evidence of the relationship. The older the case, the fewer details there are in the records. Researchers will find the name of the unwed mother, the suspected father, the child's name (only if the case occurred after the child was born), date of the case, the bond amount, the witnesses, and the judge's ruling. Some fathers were able to successfully resist paying a bastardy bond, and if so, it is recorded in court books.

How to find records of illegitimacy

These illegitimacy records are not online for any county. The Appearance docket books, also called the Continuance docket in some counties, is where these cases are recorded. Some counties have separate Bastardy Bond Indexes. In the index is a listing of the court date, mother's name, child's name(s), father's name and amount of bond. The court dockets are kept quarterly until the 1900s. When researching, be prepared with a range of quarters or years to search based on when the mother would be pregnant or with an infant. Because bastardy bonds were considered part of a criminal action, they are found in the criminal court records for the county.

Orphans

Historically the term "orphan" applied to children whose father was deceased. It was not used to describe a child whose mother died, and the father was still alive. Today we consider a child an orphan when both parents are deceased. Genealogists need to assess which definition applies in their research from the context of the records they are viewing.

The history of orphans in Pennsylvania is scarce. Philadelphia, being the largest city, of course had the most orphans. It was the landing place of hundreds of thousands of Irish- and German-speaking people fleeing famine and civil unrest from 1840 to 1850. The U.S. Civil War from 1861–1865 resulted in the deaths of over 26,000 service members from Pennsylvania. By 1870, Pennsylvania had a real issue with parentless children.

To deal with the abundance of orphan children, Philadelphia organized "orphan trains." Children were put on trains and sent to mid-Western states. There the children were put to work on farms as unpaid labor. No records survive of the children's names, but we know of these trains' existence from newspapers articles. The best estimate is 1,000 to 10,000 orphans were relocated in this way. The practice of orphan trains stopped around 1929 with the Great Depression.

Orphans of Pennsylvania's Civil War veterans had a different fate. The state built a network of orphanages providing housing, meals, and education for those children. Almost every county had a Soldier's Orphans School or Home. Orphan children were also housed with families who received funds from the state for food, clothing, and schooling (similar to what we know today as foster families).

Orphan children were also taken care of by local organizations, either coordinated by the wealthy or churches. Some examples are the Children's Aid Society, founded in Philadelphia in 1882, and the Philadelphia Society for Services to Children. Records for these two organizations survive at the Historical Society of Pennsylvania in Philadelphia. The Hershey School was founded for orphaned boys in 1909 by chocolate tycoon Milton S. Hershey and maintains its own historical records. An organization known as The Home for Friendless Children had multiple branches across Pennsylvania.

How to find records of orphanages

There is no compiled listing of all of Pennsylvania's orphanages and their surviving record locations. Part of the difficulty in obtaining these records is the Pennsylvania state law requiring that adoption records be sealed no matter how old they are. The records may exist, but the organizations holding them are keeping them private so they are not charged with a misdemeanor.

An additional challenge is orphanages changed names over the decades as they went under new management, such as from church to government funding. Researchers with orphans will do best to contact the county historical society where their orphan ancestor lived. They would be able to educate on orphanage history, local practices, and any possible surviving records.

Adoption

History and practices

Adoption of children was an informal process for most of American history. Children whose parents died, or whose parents were unable to care for them, would be taken in with another family, usually relatives. Sometimes the child informally took the family's surname (if it was not already shared). These informal adoptions usually occurred without any paperwork processed through court or church records.

For families of substantial wealth concerned with how property would be inherited, adoption was a formal process. The state legislature would pass a private law declaring a child the legal heir of an unrelated adult to formalize the adoption. Records of these private law adoptions are found in Pennsylvania legislative records and have not been sealed unlike other adoption records. Surname searches in the *Laws of Pennsylvania* book series by year, or the Pennsylvania Legislative Reference Bureau website at **https://palrb.gov** can be done for these rare adoptions. Candy Crocker Livengood's book, *Genealogical Abstracts of the Laws of Pennsylvania and the Statues at Large,* abstracts adoptions as well as other personal events from these records up to 1810.

On May 4, 1855 the Pennsylvania Assembly passed a law stating "for any person desirous of adopting any child as his or her heir...to present his or her petition to such court in the county where he or she may be resident." This was the start of adoption as a formal process through the courts, similar to what we know today. The Assembly continued to do private law adoption until 1874 when they outlawed themselves from doing so. Since 1874, child adoption is done through county courts.

Currently, Pennsylvania is a closed adoption state. This means that all adoption proceedings from any year, in any county court, are sealed. Also sealed is the original birth record of the adoptee. The adoptee's original birth record is amended to show the adoptive parents in the "Mother" and "Father" spaces (now noted as "Parent A" and "Parent B").

Since 2017, adoptees have been able to request a copy of their original birth certificate from the Pennsylvania Department of Health.

Formal adoption process

The formal adoption process currently occurs at the county level in each county's Court of Common Pleas. It is a complex process involving months of court appearances and multiple government agencies. The process detailed here began in 1905, adding layers of reviews and approvals over the decades.

If the biological parents are alive, they must formally relinquish the child, under eighteen years old, to an agency or the adoptive parents. Relinquishment could be voluntary or involuntary. The guidelines for involuntary relinquishment are detailed in state law, and include:

- Failing to perform parental duties or support the child for six months or more
- Abuse or neglect of the child
- Child is under the care of an agency and parent location is unknown
- The parent committed violent felonies such as rape, murder or sex abuse

The process of adoption creates the following records for the court files:

- The adopting parent(s) petition to the court.
- Details of the biological parents and adoptive parents, including name, age, residence, marital status, place and date of marriage, and often statements about religious affiliation, occupation, and standing in the community.
- Details of the child including name, date of birth, sex, race, age, religious affiliation, residence, siblings of the child (if any), any property the child might possess, and if represented by an

agency or institution (if they have custody of the child) or lawyer.

- The biological parents' termination of parental rights.
- The adoptive parents' investigation paperwork. Report of the home, financial status, occupation of parents, health, mental condition, and reputation in community is written up.
- In some cases, witnesses are interviewed. If a child has a guardian, they will give testimony at a hearing. All testimony in front of the judge would be in the file.
- Court records of hearing before a judge with everyone involved.
- A child who is twelve or older must give formal consent to adoption.
- The adoption decree after the Common Pleas Court Judge approves the adoption, ending the adoption process.

Once the decree is issued, the birth certificate is changed, swapping out the biological parents with the adoptive parents. The child's first name, middle name, and surname can all change.

Information collected during adoption proceedings

Access to the adoption files and decrees is limited to adoptees, biological parents, and adoptive parents. A petition to the court is necessary because adoption records are sealed in Pennsylvania. Adoptees may be able to access non-identifying information on their adoption without court order.

Adults who were adopted as children in Pennsylvania can get access to the following non-identifying information in an adoption file:

- The adopted child's birthdate and birthplace
- The ages of the birth father and mother
- Physical characteristics of the birth father and mother, such as

eye color or hair color

- The birth parents' medical history, religion, or ethnicity
- The birth parents' occupations and educational backgrounds
- The reason the birth parents placed the child for adoption
- The agency that handled the adoption

To obtain the information, an adoptee aged eighteen years old or older would contact one of the following:

- The county Court of Common Pleas for the county in which the closed adoption took place
- The private adoption agency that handled the closed adoption

Depending on the situation around the adoption, identifying information may also be available – specific details that could locate the birth parents, the adult adoptee, or other birth relatives. Identifying information may include the following:

- Names of the birth father and mother
- The birth name of the adopted child (which may be different from the name subsequently assigned to the child by the adopted parents)
- Addresses where either birth parent has lived
- Companies where either birth parent has worked
- Social security numbers of the birth parents
- Contact information of the birth parents, such as email addresses or phone numbers
- Certain types of medical information

There are restrictions around identifying information on adopted children, both those born in Pennsylvania and those born elsewhere and then adopted in Pennsylvania. The adoption agency and Department of Health work with individuals on a case-by-case basis.

How to find adoption records

Because adoption records are sealed in Pennsylvania, access through typical genealogical research methods is not an option. However, there are work arounds!

As with all genealogical work, starting by asking cousins, nieces, nephews and other family members what stories they have and what they remember. Each story may have a clue that leads to the circumstances of an adoption or biological parents. Things like home town, work the parents did, how often and where they traveled, previous marriages or other relationships – all help.

Next, look for details on death certificates and burial paperwork. Is there an unexpected informant of the death or an unknown individual who paid for the burial? This may be a biological child or parent who reconnected with deceased before death. On the birth certificate, evaluate the doctor and addresses of all involved. Do they match up with what you know of the family? Carry out a search through telephone or street directories of the time to see who lived at those addresses.

In 2017, Pennsylvania altered the adoption law to allow an adoptee or the adoptee's direct descendants to apply for his or her original birth certificate. The original birth certificate has the child's name at birth as well as the birth mother's and father's names The PA Department of Health, Office of Vital Statistics manages the application process for original birth certificates. Visit the DOH website for the latest information.

Reports from people who have applied for original birth certificates of adoptees have been mixed. Instead of sending photocopies of original birth certificates (similar to the images one would see on Ancestry of original certificates), the Department of Health is transcribing the information and typing it onto modern birth certificates. Not all the information is transcribed, and there is no way to tell how much is missing. Original certificates are the most helpful for supplying identifying information of birth parents.

A third place to search for clues is every genealogist's favorite: newspapers. It was common for adoptees to post letters or notices in newspapers looking for biological parents. Parents, particularly mothers, who gave up their parental rights would also put notices in newspapers looking for their children. Searches of keywords such an parent or child name and "seeking" or "searching" in local newspapers could reveal these notices. Sometimes assembling a timeline of events and details found in newspaper articles over the years could lead you to the biological parents.

And lastly, the supreme workaround for adoption is autosomal DNA testing. In many cases, the results of DNA tests tell of a non-expected parent event or adoption in the family line. Most researchers build out two family trees – one for the biological line and one for the adoptive line. While many people are happy to find new biological family members or to find the answers to family mysteries, some are not. The expectation of birth parents was that their identity was to always remain a secret. Tread cautiously.

Name Changes

Outside of child adoption, the most common formal surname change occurs during marriage. Women historically replaced their birth surname with their husband's surname. The second most common way surnames change is through divorce. All name changes during marriage or divorce are covered under the processes in Chapter 6 and Chapter 7.

Outside of marriage and divorce, individuals must petition their local county Court of Common Pleas to have any part of their name legally changed. These petitions go to a judge who issues a decree once completed. To locate a petition, check the Judgements Index at the county Prothonotary Office.

Of course, genealogists experience informal or accidental name changes all the time. It is common to see spelling variations with the dropping and adding of letters from surnames. There is no government process that captured or authorized these small changes. In other words, there is rarely a vital record that corrects spelling errors. Researchers must correlate all the evidence on individuals to assess whether they have the same individual with different name spellings across records, or different individuals. After the correlation, writing a summary of findings, or a genealogical proof argument, can resolve these informal name changes.

Chapter 10

Substitutes for Vital Records

THIS CHAPTER LISTS RECORDS that can be used as a substitute for the types of information found in vital records. Most of these records can also be used to confirm and enhance information in vital records.

This my personal "go-to" list and other genealogists will have additional suggestions. Use whatever historical records you can get to find answers to your genealogical research questions.

Ideas on how to use each type of record to calculate birth and death dates is included, along with places to find the records.

Funeral Home Records

Today funeral homes are where the recently deceased were embalmed, prepared for burial, or cremated. The first funeral homes in Pennsylvania was founded in 1761 with a focus on making coffins.[1] For the next hundred years, coffin-making remained the funeral home's main purpose. Preparing the deceased for viewing and burial was done by family members, and services were led by religious leaders. It was not until the last half of the nineteenth century that funeral homes became what we know of today. These businesses began in the state's largest cities - Philadelphia, Reading, Allentown, Scranton, Harrisburg, and Pittsburgh – before appearing in smaller cities and towns.

Funeral home records always have the name of the deceased, date of death, and disposition of the body (burial, cremation, or donation of cadaver for science). Often the closest family members are listed, along with residence and religious faith. The Genealogical Society of Pennsylvania and the Historical Society of Pennsylvania have collections from the Philadelphia-area. In other counties check the historical society. A full list is in Appendix D: Archives with Historical Records. The FamilySearch catalog and Ancestry also host digital images of some funeral homes, often defunct ones.

Burial Records

Burials occurred in church or synagogue graveyards, private non-denominational cemeteries, family cemeteries (on private land), or pauper cemeteries. For those who were cremated, there may be burial records for the cremains, or the ashes could have been scattered. In cities, permits were required to bury the recently deceased. Philadelphia began keeping these records in 1803. Scranton, Reading, Bethlehem, Allentown, Harrisburg, and Pittsburgh also had stricter rules on burials than rural areas.

Burials records involve two sets of books: burial plot books, which list the owners of the spaces in the cemetery; and interment books, which list who was buried in each space. While researchers can search for both sets of books, the interment book is the more valuable one for obtaining vital record information.

A word of caution about the well-known memorial websites FindAGrave and BillionGraves – it is possible for people to create memorial pages in cemeteries with no confirmation of the burial happening. If any website lists a burial in a cemetery, the burial should be verified with either a headstone or the cemetery's interment book information.

To find or verify burial information, contact the organization managing the cemetery. For a church or synagogue graveyard, you may need to trace the history of the congregation to find the records. Private non-denominational cemeteries usually have an office with records you can request. Pauper cemeteries are managed by the county and the coroner's office would be the point of contact for those records. Family cemeteries on private land are the hardest records to find.

Local genealogical and historical societies have usually transcribed these headstones for researchers. See Appendix D: Archives with Historical Records for a listing of these organizations. Most homeowners do not want people walking around their yards to find these tiny cemeteries, so start with the local societies first.

Probate Records

Probate is the process of distributing the deceased's assets after death. Probate occurs whether a person has a will (detailed instructions for distribution of assets) or no will, also known as intestate, as long as the deceased assets meet the threshold amount for probate. Pennsylvania counties often use the terms "estate file" or "estate administration" instead of probate.

Beginning in 1874, an estate could not enter probate without proof of death, specifying the place and date of death, and occasionally the deceased's age or birth date. The form of this proof varied by county, but it should be in the probate documents among the loose papers. By state law, the deceased's estate would be distributed to the spouse and children, unless the deceased specified otherwise. Sometimes siblings and parents are mentioned in wills and in the probate process.

The Register of Wills in each county holds the files of the estates probated through that county. People who died intestate had their estate processed through the Orphans' Court, but once the estate is distributed to heirs, the files are transferred to the Register of Wills. In many counties will books and estate administration indexes have been microfilmed by FamilySearch. Rarely have the entire estate (probate) proceedings been made available online. For genealogy research, the entire file is necessary. Contact the county courthouse where the person lived to obtain copies of the full probate file. A full listing of courthouses is in Appendix C: Government Sources for Vital Records.

Guardianship Records

A guardian is a substitute parent for a child under the age of full adulthood. Today, eighteen is considered adulthood, but historically, full age of adulthood was twenty-one years old. Persons between eighteen and twenty-one would need an adult to co-sign on legal documents, but otherwise they were capable of being independent.

In the nineteenth century and earlier, a guardian was appointed if the father died and the father owned property. At that time, a child was considered an orphan if the father died, even if the mother was still alive. If the mother died and the father was still alive, no guardian was appointed. If both parents died and they owned property, a guardian could be appointed, but in most cases the land was sold and the proceeds held until the children reached the age of eighteen.

The court-appointed guardian would report to the county Orphans' Court quarterly on the status of the property in care. The guardian did this until the oldest male child turned twenty-one. The Orphans' Court records detail the date of death of parent(s), ages of the children, family relationships, amount and type of assets, and the quarterly updates on the family's wealth. As with probate records, full files are not available for viewing online. Contact the county courthouse where the family resided to obtain the full file. All the courthouses are listed in Appendix C: Government Sources for Vital Records.

Note: The Orphans' Court was not named this way because it is dealing only with these cases of orphaned children needing guardians. The name "Orphans Court" refers to the assortment of court cases it takes on that fall outside civil matters or criminal cases.

Family Bibles

Families would often write the birth, marriage, and death dates of their family members in the front pages of their Bible. These Bibles were often passed down, mother to daughter, over generations. Researchers looking for these might find them today with their second, third, or fourth cousins. However, most people today do not know family extended out to that many levels of cousins, and so a second place to look is in archives.

Many family Bibles in archives are usually at least 150 years old. Their frail condition mean the pages with genealogy information have been photocopied or microfilmed. Local historical and genealogical societies often have copies of these Bible pages. See the listing of these organizations in Appendix D: Archives with Historical Records. Lineage societies such as Daughters of the American Revolution and Sons of the American Revolution, also keep copies of Bible pages in their member applications.

Newspapers

Few things have transformed genealogy research as much as digital newspapers and OCR (Optical Character Recognition). OCR allows websites to "read" the letters on digital images and translate them into searchable text. OCR is not 100 percent perfect, but it is much faster than reading newspapers one page at a time on microfilm reels.

With digital images of newspapers and OCR, it is easy to search thousands of newspapers for births, marriages, and deaths. Sadly, only a small percentage of Pennsylvania newspapers have been digitized compared to the total number published. To determine all the available titles of local county newspapers, contact the local county genealogical society. Find the one you want in Appendix D: Archives with Historical Records. County genealogical societies often have volunteer-made indexes of obituaries and other mentions of death and marriage, created in the days before digital images and OCR. These indexes can fill the gap of what OCR has missed due to the way it (mis)reads pages.

State and Federal Military Records

Military pension records are filled with details of service members and their families. It is common to find spouses' and children's names, dates of birth, places of birth, and dates of death or if a pension was paid. Prior to the Civil War, records are not as complete, but service members' ages and birth places were often provided.

Entire books and websites have been written on military records and locating them by time period and type of service. Start with the National Archives for Army, Air Force, Coast Guard, Navy, and Marine records. For Pennsylvania militia records, the Pennsylvania State Archives would be the best starting place. Their contact information is in Appendix C: Government Sources for Vital Records.

For Pennsylvania researchers, one easily accessible set of records is the Pennsylvania Veterans Compensation Application Files, now digitized on Ancestry, and organized by war. The state paid a small financial amount to residents who served in war time. Files detail the applicant's date of birth, as well as the age of spouse and children.

Naturalization and Immigration Records

Like military records, an entire book could be written on how to locate naturalization and immigration records in Pennsylvania. The laws and forms used to record new arrivals through the ports of Philadelphia and Erie (plus nearby New York City and Baltimore) often changed. In brief, it was not until 1810 that immigrant names were recorded by the federal government for all ethnicities. It took until the 1840s for names and ages to be listed on ship passenger lists consistently. Both Philadelphia and Erie arrivals are archived at the National Archives in Philadelphia and digitized on either Ancestry or FamilySearch (depending on the year).

The first part of the process for citizenship, the Declaration of Intention, required the person's age. This is very helpful when so many family members arrived with similar names, the age listing can help distinguish them. The final step, Petition for Naturalization, also required age and/or date of birth. The home residence or birthplace are stated more often after the 1880s. By 1910, its consistently entered on the forms.

The majority of pre-twentieth century naturalization records are in county courthouses and state court records. See Appendix C: Government Sources for Vital Records for a listing of courthouses. It was also possible to naturalize through federal courts, although these were located in Philadelphia and Pittsburgh for most of the state's history so not easily accessible for the majority. The federal government took over naturalization in 1906, and those records, along with all previous federal records are in the National Archives in Philadelphia.

Adding to the complexity, online indexes for immigration and naturalization do not include complete record sets across all three levels of government: federal, state, and local. Researchers must search each level to do an exhaustive search.

State Asylum and Prisoner Records

Starting in the late nineteenth century, the state of Pennsylvania opened asylums for mental health, sanatoriums for chronic diseases, and prisons or penitentiaries for convicted criminals. The people in these state institutions were called inmates or patients depending on the facility. Included on institution intake forms are names, dates of birth or age, place of birth, family members, and detailed family histories.

Many of these state institutions are now closed. The Pennsylvania State Archive has been working to collect records and preserve them. Contact the Pennsylvania State Archives in Harrisburg for details of how to obtains copies of these records. Their information is in Appendix C: Government Sources for Vital Records.

Note: Some of the words used to describe the people, their actions, and their conditions in these institutions are considered offensive now. Sensitive researchers may choose to avoid these records entirely.

Mortality Schedules of the United States Census

The mortality schedule was part of the U.S. Census in 1850, 1860, 1870, 1880, and 1885 in selected U.S. territories. The federal government used it to assess death rates and causes prior to the implementation of death certificates in states. The U.S. mortality schedules for Pennsylvania survived intact. (Not every location was as fortunate.)

The mortality schedules include:

- Deceased's name
- Sex
- Age
- Color
- Whether widowed
- Place of birth
- Month in which the death occurred
- Profession, occupation, or trade
- Disease or cause of death
- Number of days ill
- Parents' birthplaces (1870 only)
- Place disease contracted and residency length (1880 only)

Ancestry has indexed the original images in "U.S., Federal Census Mortality Schedules, 1850–1885," found online at **https://www.ancestry.com/search/collections/8756/.**

Business Records

In each county of Pennsylvania there were businesses and industries which were central to the local economy. It could have been an iron furnace, a steel mill, a railroad, a coal mine, or a factory producing textiles, cigars, or home goods. Records that remain of these places vary, but it is worth checking local historical societies and college libraries in the ancestor's area. Sometimes, the record keepers for these businesses recorded details of their employees, such as age, place of birth, and if they needed time off for marriage or death in the family.

The most efficient way to research these records is to note the occupations of ancestors in the family tree. Occupations are noted on census records and tax records. Use historical maps to locate businesses around where ancestors lived. If they were noted as an "iron worker," what industry marked around them on the map would be working with iron? The process applies for ancestors who worked with the railroad, steel factories, and textile mills.

Once the names of the businesses and their locations have been determined, contact the local archives. Sometimes local history organizations or archives have business ledgers, correspondence, or collected scrapbooks of information. Appendix D: Archives with Historical Records gives you a starting point. This type of research is not easy, but it may be necessary when researching early Pennsylvania ancestors due to the scarcity of other records.

---

1. "Our History," Kirk & Nice Funeral Home (https://www.kirkandniceinc.com/our-history). The historical records of Kirk & Nice were microfilmed by FamilySearch in 2006.

Appendix A: Common Terms Found in Vital Records

Affidavit: Written facts completed on a form or other document. Created in front of a court officer or notary public, and sworn under oath. Often provided in the days before standard identification to verify identity or age of a person.

Age of Consent: The age at which a person can marry without parental or guardian consent. In Pennsylvania the age of consent was twenty-one until 1972 when it was changed to eighteen.

Age of Contractability: The age below which a person could not be legally married with or without parental or guardian consent. Also known as the minimum age for marriage. Pennsylvania set the minimum age for marriage at sixteen years old in 1872.

Age of Majority: The age at which a person is considered old enough to handle their own affairs. Historically, this has been twenty-one years old for males, and eighteen years old for females for all areas of life. In contemporary times, the age varies not by gender, but by activity.

Annulment: Retroactive invalidation of marriage between two individuals. Annulment can be done through the courts or through a religious group, but it most commonly refers to a process through the Roman Catholic Church of nullifying a marriage. An annulled marriage is a marriage that never occurred.

Attestation: Testimony given in regards to family status, residence, citizenship, employment, or ownership, and given under oath and signed by witnesses.

Bastardy Bond: Sometimes called a "bastardly bond." A monetary bond issued by a county or state court to the father of a child born out of marriage. The money collected was used to ensure the child would be financially supported. A child born outside of marriage was also referred to as "illegitimate." The term "bastard" as well as "illegitimate" were legal terms and are considered offensive today. They are no longer used in Pennsylvania state law.

Bed and Board: Historical term used to refer to a legal separation of a marriage, rather than a completed divorce through the legal system. Also called "*a mensa et thoro*." This wording could be found within the court records of a couple going through divorce proceedings.

Certified Birth Certificate or Certified Death Certificate: A copy of the original certificate created by the Department of Health on official paper with a raised seal. Must be ordered for any birth or death certificate that is not in the publicly available years on file at the Pennsylvania State Archives.

Children's Aid Societies: Private programs established by wealthy benefactors or religious groups to care for poor children. Usually found in cities in Pennsylvania from about 1870 through 1960. These private societies were largely replaced by government programs administered by the state.

Cohabitation: A single man and a single woman living together in one household, acting as husband and wife.

Consanguinity: Relatedness of one person to another through a common ancestor. Each religion and each state defines the degree of relatedness allowed for marriage.

Consent Affidavit: Consent provided by a parent or legal guardian of an underage bride or groom. Filed with the marriage license application. The age of consent differed by time period and location. In Pennsylvania, the age of consent was twenty-one until 1972 when it was changed to eighteen.

Court-Appointed Guardian: An adult assigned by the local county civil court to care for a minor child. Historically guardians were appointed only for unrelated children with significant wealth who did not have other family members available to look after their assets. The majority of children without parents prior to about 1940 went to orphanages or extended family members.

Decedent: A person who is dead, no longer living.

Divorce Decree: Legal dissolution of a marriage. Divorce in Pennsylvania is a multi-step process with petitions, waiting periods, and affidavits. Final decision – the decree – is granted by a judge in court.

Emancipated Child: A child free from parental or guardian control and able to keep own earnings and sign contracts such as property deeds and leases.

Freeman: A white male over twenty-one years of age. Freemen paid taxes, could own land, and could vote in elections.

Free Man of Color: A black man over twenty-one years of age who was either freed from enslavement or indenture, or who was free since birth. Free men of color could pay taxes and own land, but could not vote in Pennsylvania until 1870.

Full Age: A person who reached adult age, twenty-one years old historically.

Guardian: A person appointed by the local county civil court to make decisions on behalf of another person, usually a minor under eighteen years old. Guardians were also appointed for adults who a court determined (historical terms) were incompetent, disabled (invalid), or mentally disabled (idiotic).

Lineal: A direct biological relationship of parent to child, either male or female.

Marriage License Application: The bride and groom (now partner one and partner two) applied to a clerk of the Orphans' Court or head of the Marriage License Bureau for permission to marry. Requirements differed by time period. Without approval by the county government, couples were not permitted to marry.

Marriage Banns: Announcement of intent to marry done three times prior to marriage. These were not practiced in Pennsylvania but did occur in Ireland, England, and Scotland, the nationalities of many of the colonists.

Marriage Bond: Posted by a family member of the bride, usually showing a large amount of money and stating the intended marriage. A few bonds can be found in Pennsylvania colonial county records but they were a practice only of the very wealthy.

Marriage Certificate: Normally given to the couple at the time of marriage or after filing by a civil official. There are no copies of marriage certificates in county records. Sometimes they can be found in pension records because the surviving spouse provided a copy in the application process.

Marriage License: Permission from the county's clerk of the Orphans' Court to allow the legal union between two people. A marriage license duplicate certificate is presented to a minister or official to conduct the marriage.

Marriage Return: The final step of the marriage process. The minister or official signs the marriage license duplicate certificate that marriage was completed and returns it to the courthouse. This duplicate certificate, on file at the courthouse, is the marriage return.

Midwife: A woman experienced in childbirth and delivering babies who helps other women during birth. This was an unlicensed and informally trained profession for most of American history. Midwives delivered more babies than physicians until about the 1910s.

Miscegenation: The marriage of two people of different races. Pennsylvania did not have a state law against marriage of different races, ethnicities, or religions.

Natural Child: The child of a couple who are not married. The couple may also be unable to be married legally under the current state laws.

Natural Guardian: An adult who is responsible for the health and well-being of a minor child, regardless of the financial resources of that child. This is typically the parent-child relationship. It can also be extended family such as aunts, uncles, and grandparents caring for the child.

Next Friend: A person who acts on behalf of another person who is unable to act for themselves. This person is not formally a legal guardian, but acts in that role for a minor or an adult viewed as incompetent.

Orphans' Court: Pennsylvania civil court organized at the county level with jurisdiction over the following cases: intestate proceedings (deceased individuals without wills), guardianships for minor children, and issuance of marriage licenses.

Posthumous Child: A child who was born after the death of the father.

Private Law: A law passed by the legislature and signed by the governor for the benefit of the just the persons listed in the legislation. Commonly used in the nineteenth century and earlier to divorce married couples, resolve property disputes, and award military pensions. The ability to pass private laws ended with the passage of 1881 Pennsylvania Constitution.

Prothonotary: The clerk of courts for a county. He or she is responsible for maintaining county court filings in docket books. Prothonotary is an elected position.

Spinster: An unmarried woman who lives independently. In the past this was mostly widows. Could also refer to a woman who spins wool into yarn.

Waiver: The intentional and voluntary surrender of one's own legal rights. It is stated on a document signed by the person with witnesses.

Appendix B: Selected Pennsylvania Laws Relating to Vital Records

A SUMMARY OF EACH state law is provided along with a citation of the law.

When citing Pennsylvania laws, the following format applies: A citation for the Pamphlet Laws for sessions in 1826 and earlier is written "act of April 10, 1826 (P.L.235, Ch.130)." A citation for the Pamphlet Laws for sessions in 1827 and later is written "act of January 16, 1827 (P.L.9, No.10)."

Marriage and Divorce

1701

Act of October 28, 1701 (1 Sm.L.160,Ch.109) Act for the preventing of clandestine marriages. Parents or guardians consent should be obtained prior to marriage. Marriages are to occur before a Justice of the Peace, unless they occur in a religious society. Servants are not permitted to marry without master's approval. Twelve witnesses required for all marriages. Fines of five to twenty pounds for couple, and each marriage witness for violations.

1730

Act of October 28, 1730 (1 Sm.L.311,Ch.311) Supplement to an act for the preventing of clandestine marriages. No marriages permitted of non-residents of cities or counties, minors, or indentured servants. Fines increased to fifty pounds.

1871

Act of June 2, 1871 (P.L.269) "Relating to clandestine marriages" No justice of the peace, clergyman, minister or other person who performs marriages shall be liable for the penalty of joining in marriage persons under age twenty-one unless they disregard provisions of first section of 1729 act.

1874

Pennsylvania Constitution of 1874, Article III, Section 7 The General Assembly shall not pass any local or special law granting divorces.

1885

Act of June 23, 1885 (PL.115) "Relating to marriage licenses" defined the exact form and process to be used in marriages license applications to county orphans' courts. Marriage licenses to begin October 1, 1885. Penalty for unlawful issue of a marriage license up to $1,000 per violation. Fine of $50 to ministers not returning duplicate certificates, as well as $50 fine to clerk for not recording marriage properly. Anyone solemnizing a marriage of a couple without a marriage license to be fined $100 per illegal marriage. Pamphlet Law 115 also repealed section 2 of the Clandestine Marriage act of 1730.

1891

Act of June 1, 1891 (P.L.130) Amended "An Act Concerning Divorce" of 1884 to provide an additional cause for divorce within the state. If either spouse was convicted of felony in or out of state with a prison sentence of two years or more, a divorce could be petitioned to the courts.

Act of June 8, 1891 (P.L. 207) Extended the jurisdiction of divorce to wives who were born in the state, but moved out of state and returned to live in the commonwealth. The husband continued to live outside of Pennsylvania. Reasons for leaving her husband and filing for divorce included "his cruel and barbarous treatment or of such indignities to a person as to render her condition intolerable and her life burdensome, or willful or malicious desertion and absence from the habitation of the other without a reasonable cause."

Act of June 11, 1891 (P.L. 222) Either party in an ongoing divorce proceeding or one that is being appealed, can now file with their county Prothonotary.

1893

Act of May 1, 1893 (P.L.24) Required that Clerk of the Orphans' Court, either where the couple resided or where the marriage performed, identify one or both of the applicants. Licenses issued in any Pennsylvania county good in all counties. Duplicate licenses to be returned to the county where the marriage was solemnized. Law effective October 1, 1895.

Act of June 20, 1893 (P.L.342) A supplement to "An act extending the jurisdiction of the courts of this Commonwealth in cases of divorce" allowed divorce proceedings to occur in the courts of common pleas. Effective immediately for all divorce proceeding currently in the courts. Act of June 8, 1891 entitled "A further supplement to an act entitled 'An act extending the jurisdiction of the courts of this Commonwealth in cases of divorce,'" is repealed.

1913

Act No. 64 and Act No. 65 both of April 17, 1913 Repeal the act for the preventing clandestine marriages of October 28, 1701 and February 14, 1730.

Act No. 458 of July 24, 1913 (P.L. 1013) Licenses to marry are only issued by the Clerk of the Orphans' Court. The marriage license application shall be uniform throughout the state and the DOH will set the standard form. No license will be issued to imbeciles, epileptics, anyone of unsound mind, or any male who was an inmate at an asylum or home for indigent person within the last five years. No licenses issued to people who are intoxicated or under the influence of drugs at the time of application. License is good for sixty days from date of issue.

1972

Act No. 152 of June 16, 1972 (H.B. 1715) Marriage age changed from twenty-one years with parent or guardian approval to eighteen years old and no parent or guardian approval required.

1976

Act No. 214 of October 7, 1976 (S.B. 1148) Repeal of marriage license restrictions begun in 1913 on people who were inmates at asylums or indigent homes.

1980

Act No. 1980-26 of April 2, 1980 (H.B. 640) Takes effect in ninety days. Consolidation of divorce laws in the "Divorce Code" and beginning of no-fault divorce in the Commonwealth. Divorce decrees still processed through county prothonotary.

1990

Act No. 1990-206 of December 19, 1990 (H.B. 1023) Takes effect in ninety days. Further consolidation of marriage, adoption, divorce laws into the Consolidated Statutes, Title 23: Domestic Relations.

1993

Act No. 1993-79 of December 22, 1993 (H.B. 1432) Takes effect in sixty days. The delineator of "race" is removed from marriage license applications.

2004

Act No. 204-144 of November 23, 2004 (H.B. 2719) Effective January 1, 2005. Amends Consolidated Statue § 1103 on common law marriage. "No common-law marriage contracted after January 1, 2005, shall be valid. Nothing in this part shall be deemed or taken to render any common-law marriage otherwise lawful and contracted on or before January 1, 2005, invalid."

Birth and Death Records

1860

Act No. 146 of March 8, 1860 Entitled "For the registration of Births, Marriages, and Deaths in the city of Philadelphia" All clergymen, magistrates, physicians, midwives, undertakers, and cemetery caretakers must provide their name and address to the health officer for the city. Beginning July 1, 1860, the health officer of the city shall keep separate books for births, marriages, and deaths. Each February the health officer to report to city council the totals of each. Physicians and the coroner to complete and submit a death certificate within forty-eight hours of the death to the undertaker. Undertaker to add the occupation of deceased along with place of birth, street address, ward number, place of

1874

Act No. 127 of May 15, 1874 (P.L.127) All persons applying for letters testamentary or letters of administration to the register of wills must supply an affidavit of the decedent's day and hour of death.

1893

Act of No. 281 of June 6, 1893 (P.L.281) The clerk of the Orphans'

Court of each county to keep record of all births and death occurring in their county. When a minor, the name of the father and mother also recorded. Tax assessors in townships and boroughs are to collect the information twice a year from parents and guardians. The clerk of the Orphans' Court to receive 5 cents for each name recorded. Tax assessors also to receive 5 cents for each name collected. Any person who violates the provisions of the act shall pay $10 for each offense. Law not applicable in cities where a registration system for births and deaths already exists.

1905

Act No. 218 of April 27, 1905 Created a Department of Health (DOH) and defining its powers and duties. The DOH is responsible for registration of births, marriages, and deaths. The state is apportioned into ten vital record registration districts, each run by an officer appointed by the Commissioner. Persons who violate any order from the DOH or interfere with performance of its duties are charged with a misdemeanor and fined up to $100 or imprisoned up to one month.

Adoption

1855

Act No. 456 of May 4, 1855 (P.L.430) Mothers have all the same rights for children as fathers have. Children adopted can change their surname to their adoptive parents surname as part of the adoption decree issued by court.

1872

Act No. 20 of April 2, 1872 (P.L.31) A supplement to the 1855 law above. When the common law form of adopting a child is done, it will be recorded in the Recorder of Deeds office.

1874

Pennsylvania Constitution of 1874, Article III, Section 7 The General Assembly shall not pass any local or special law authorizing the adoption of legitimation of children, or changing the names of person or places,

1905

Act No. 208 of April 22, 1905 Amends previous laws. If the adopting parent has other children, the adopted child shall share inheritance equally with the other children. Parent(s) of the child available for adoption must consent to the adoption.

1982

Act No. 1982-174 of June 23, 1982 (H.B.1789) Takes effect in one year. Amends Consolidated Statute § 2909 to remove all identifying information of a child adoptee's natural (birth) family from birth records. Court adoption records are made private beginning in 1984.

Appendix C: Government Sources for Vital Records

THIS SECTION IS DIVIDED into three sources of vital records and vital record substitutes: government offices, company or organization websites, and private organizations. To understand when to use each place, read the accompanying chapter for the record type. Records can be available in their original form on paper (or in a digital image) or only transcribed, with no image or original available.

Listed first are the state level offices, followed by the county level offices. More and more counties have created a separate archive building for their historical records. Which years and types of records are stored in the county archive vs the main county administrative building varies by county. In addition, Pennsylvania state law allows local governments to transfer historical records to museums, libraries, and archives. This varies county-to-county, so researchers should verify record locations and access before visiting in-person.

State Level

For certified, non-public birth certificates and death certificates:

Pennsylvania Department of Health, Division of Vital Records
Website: https://www.health.pa.gov/topics/certificates

Note: Ordering is through the DOH website. Rules for ordering birth certificates and death certificates varies and protects the privacy of living people. There are no longer "non-certified" certificates available for genealogy research.

For original, publicly available birth certificates and death certificates (Some years found on Ancestry. See Chapters 3 and 4 for details):

Pennsylvania State Archives
1681 North Sixth Street
Harrisburg, PA 17120-0090
Telephone: (717) 783-3281
Email: ra-statearchives@pa.gov
Website: https://pastatearchives.com
Catalog: https://www.phmc.pa.gov/Archives/Research-Online

County Level

For county marriage license applications, birth registrations, and death registrations, contact the county courthouse of residence at the time of the vital record event. Some of the counties have archives where they hold records older than the last few decades, and these historical vital records will be there, rather than the courthouse.

Tip: To find if a county has any information online for genealogists, type "genealogy" in the search box on its website. Genealogists are the most frequent researchers to courthouses and many counties have provided information for them.

Adams County

County of Adams
117 Baltimore Street
Gettysburg, PA 17325
Phone: (717)334-6781
Website: https://www.adamscountypa.gov

***

Allegheny County

Allegheny County Office Building
542 Forbes Avenue
Pittsburgh, PA 15219
Phone: (412)350-4636
Website: https://www.alleghenycounty.us

***

Armstrong County

Armstrong County Courthouse
500 E. Market Street
Suite 102
Kittanning, PA 16201
Phone: (724)548-3236
Website: http://www.co.armstrong.pa.us

***

Beaver County

Beaver County Courthouse
810 Third Street
Beaver, PA 15009
Phone: (724)728-5700
Website: https://www.beavercountypa.gov

***

Bedford County

Bedford County Courthouse
200 South Juliana Street
Bedford, PA 15522
Phone: (724)728-5700
Website: https://www.bedfordcountypa.org

***

Berks County

Berks County Courthouse
633 Court Street
Reading, PA 19601
Phone: (610) 478-6970
Website: https://www.countyofberks.com
Berks County Government Archives coming in 2024

***

Blair County

Blair County Courthouse
423 Allegheny Street
Hollidaysburg, PA 16648
Phone: (814) 693-3000
Website: https://www.blairco.org

***

Bradford County

Bradford County Courthouse
301 Main Street
Towanda, PA 18848
Phone: (570) 265-1727
Website: https://bradfordcountypa.org

***

Bucks County

Bucks County Courthouse
Archive Center, 3rd Floor
55 East State Street
Doylestown, PA 18901
Phone: (215)348-6000
Website: https://www.buckscounty.gov

***

Butler County

Butler County Government Center
124 West Diamond Street
Butler, PA 16003
Phone: (724) 284-1409
Website: https://www.butlercountypa.gov

***

Cambria County

Cambria County Courthouse
200 South Center Street
Ebensburg, PA 15931
Phone: (814) 472-5440
Website: https://www.cambriacountypa.gov

***

Cameron County

Cameron County Courthouse
20 East Fifth Street
Emporium, PA 15834
Phone: (814) 486-3349
Website: https://www.cameroncountypa.com

***

Carbon County

Carbon County Administration Building
2 Hazard Square
Jim Thorpe, PA 18229
Phone: (570) 325-2651
Website: https://www.carboncountypa.gov

***

Centre County

Willowbank County Office Building
414 Homes Street, Suite #2
Bellefonte, PA 16823
Phone: (814) 355-6724
Website: https://www.centrecountypa.gov

***

Chester County

Chester County Archives and Records
601 Westtown Road, Suite 080
West Chester, PA 19380
Phone: (610) 344-6760
Website: https://www.chesco.org/192/Archives-Records

Chester County Courthouse
313 West Market Street
West Chester, PA 19380
Phone: (610) 334-6330
Website: https://www.chesco.org

***

Clarion County

Clarion County Administration Office
330 Main Street
Clarion, PA 16214
Phone: (814) 226-4000
Website: https://www.co.clarion.pa.us

***

Clearfield County

Clearfield County Courthouse
1 North Second Street
Clearfield, PA 16830
Phone: (814) 765-2641
Website: https://clearfieldco.org

***

Clinton County

Clinton County Courthouse
2 Piper Way
Lock Haven, PA 17745
Phone: (570) 893-4010
Website: https://www.clintoncountypa.gov

***

Columbia County

Columbia County Courthouse
35 West Main Street
Bloomsburg, PA 17815
Phone: (570) 389-5614
Website: http://www.columbiapa.org

***

Crawford County

Crawford County Courthouse
903 Diamond Park
Meadville, PA 16355
Phone: (814) 373-2537
Website:
https://www.crawfordcountypa.net/Pages/Home.aspx

***

Cumberland County

County of Cumberland
1 Courthouse Square
Carlisle, PA 17013
Phone: (717) 240-6100
Website: https://www.cumberlandcountypa.gov

***

Dauphin County

Dauphin County Courthouse
101 Market Street
Harrisburg, PA 17101
Phone: (717) 780-6500
Website: https://www.dauphincounty.gov

***

Delaware County

Archives of Delaware County
340 North Middletown Road, Building 19
Lima, PA 19063
Phone: (610) 891-5620
Website:
https://delconew.azurewebsites.net/departments/archives.html

Delaware County Government Center Complex
201 West Front Street
Media, PA 19063
Phone: (610) 891-4000
Website: https://www.delcopa.gov

***

Elk County

Elk County Courthouse
240 Main Street
Ridgeway, PA 15853
Phone: (814) 776-5349
Website: http://www.co.elk.pa.us

***

Erie County

Erie County Courthouse
140 West Sixth Street
Erie, PA 16501
Phone: (814) 451-6237
Website: https://www.eriecountypa.gov

***

Fayette County

Fayette County Courthouse
61 East Main Street
Uniontown, PA 15401
Phone: (724) 430-1238
Website: https://www.fayettecountypa.org

***

Forest County

Forest County Courthouse
240 Main Street
Tionesta, PA 16353
Phone: (814) 755-3537
Website: https://www.co.forest.pa.us

***

Franklin County

Franklin County Archives Annex
625 Franklin Farms Lane
Chambersburg, PA 17202
Phone: (717) 261-3154
Website:
https://franklincountypa.gov/index.php?section=government-archives

Franklin County Courthouse
340 North Second Street
Chambersburg, PA 17202
Phone: (717) 264-4125
Website: https://www.franklincountypa.gov

***

Fulton County

Fulton County Courthouse
201 North Second Street
McConnellsburg, PA 17233
Phone: (814) 755-3537
Website: https://www.co.fulton.pa.us

***

Greene County

Greene County Courthouse
93 East High Street
Waynesburg, PA 15370
Phone: (724) 852-5399
Website: https://www.co.greene.pa.us

***

Huntingdon County

Huntingdon County Courthouse
223 Penn Street
Huntingdon, PA 16652
Phone: (814) 643-2740
Website: https://huntingdoncountycourt.net

***

Indiana County

Indiana County Court Administration
825 Philadelphia Street
Indiana, PA 15701
Phone: (724) 465-3805
Website: https://www.indianacountypa.gov/

***

Jefferson County

Jefferson County Courthouse
200 Main Street
Brookville, PA 15825
Phone: (814) 849-1610
Website: https://www.jeffersoncountypa.com

***

Juniata County

Juniata County Courthouse
Bridge & Main Streets, P.O. Box 68
Mifflintown, PA 17059
Phone: (724) 465-3805
Website:https://www.juniataco.org

***

Lackawanna County

Lackawanna County Government Center
123 Wyoming Ave
Scranton, PA 18503
Phone: (570) 963-6702
Website: https://www.lackawannacounty.org

***

Lancaster County

Lancaster County Archives
150 North Queen Street, Suite 10
Lancaster, PA 17603
Phone: (717) 299-8319
Website: https://co.lancaster.pa.us/127/Archives-Division

Lancaster County Government Center
150 North Queen Street
Lancaster, PA 17603
Phone: (717) 299-8000
Website: https://co.lancaster.pa.us

***

Lawrence County

Lawrence County Government Center
430 Court Street
New Castle, PA 16101
Phone: (724) 658-2541
Website: https://lawrencecountypa.gov

***

Lebanon County

Lebanon County Courthouse
400 South 8th Street
Lebanon, PA 17042
Phone: (717) 274-8094
Website: https://lebanoncountypa.gov

***

Lehigh County

Lehigh County Courthouse
455 Hamilton Street
Allentown, PA 18101
Phone: (610) 782-3000
Website: https://www.lehighcounty.org

***

Luzerne County

Luzerne County Courthouse
200 North River Street
Wilkes-Barre, PA 18711
Phone: (570)825-1641
Website: https://www.luzernecounty.org

***

Lycoming County

Lycoming County Courthouse
48 West Third Street
Williamsport, PA 17701
Phone: (570) 327-2251
Website: https://www.lyco.org

***

McKean County

McKean County Courthouse
500 West Main Street
Smethport, PA 16749
Phone: (814) 887-3260
Website: https://www.mckeancountypa.gov

***

Mercer County

County of Mercer
138 South Diamond Street
Mercer, PA 16137
Phone: (724) 662-3800
Website: https://www.mercercountypa.gov/

***

Mifflin County

County of Mifflin
20 North Wayne Street
Lewistown, PA 17044
Phone: (717) 248-6733
Website: https://mifflinco.org

***

Monroe County

Monroe County Archive
One Quaker Plaza
Stroudsburg, PA 18360
Phone: (570) 517-3400
Website:
https://www.monroecountypa.gov/departments/archives

***

Montgomery County

Montgomery County Archive
86 Eagleville Road
Eagleville PA 19403
Phone: (610) 278- 3441
Website:
https://www.montgomerycountypa.gov/418/Archival-Record-Retrieval

Montgomery County Courthouse
493 Swede Street
Norristown, PA 19401
Phone: (610) 278-3000
Website: https://www.montgomerycountypa.gov

***

Montour County

Montour County Courthouse
253 Mill Street
Danville, PA 17821
Phone: (570) 271-3012
Website: https://montourcounty.gov

***

Northampton County

Northampton County Courthouse
669 Washington Street
Easton, PA 18042
Phone: (610) 829-6500
Website:
https://www.northamptoncounty.org/Pages/default.aspx

***

Northumberland County

Northumberland County Courthouse
201 Market Street
Sunbury, PA 17801
Phone: (570) 988-4148
Website: https://www.norrycopa.net

***

Perry County

Perry County Courthouse
2 East Main Street
New Bloomfield, PA 17068
Phone: (717) 582-2131
Website: https://perryco.org

***

Philadelphia

Philadelphia City Archives
548 Spring Garden Street
Philadelphia, PA 19123
Phone: (215) 685 - 9409
Website:
https://www.phila.gov/departments/department-of-records/city-archives/

Philadelphia City Hall
Broad & Market Streets
Philadelphia, PA 19107
Phone: (215) 686 - 4252
Website: https://www.phila.gov

***

Pike County

Pike County Courthouse
506 Broad Street
Milford, PA 18337
Phone: (570) 296-7231
Website: https://www.pikepa.org

***

Potter County

Potter County Courthouse
1 Main Street
Coudersport, PA 16915
Phone: (814) 274-8290
Website: https://pottercountypa.net

***

Schuylkill County

Schuylkill County Courthouse Archives
401 North 2nd Street
Pottsville, PA 17801
Phone: (570) 628-1145
Website:
https://schuylkillcountypa.gov/departments/courts___legal/archives.php

***

Snyder County

Snyder County Courthouse
9 West Market Street
Middleburg, PA 17842
Phone: (570) 837-4224
Website: https://www.snydercounty.org

***

Somerset County

Somerset County Courthouse
111 East Union Street
Somerset, PA 15501
Phone: (814) 445-1548
Website: http://www.co.somerset.pa.us

***

Sullivan County

Sullivan County Courthouse
245 Muncy Street
Laporte, PA 18626
Phone: (570) 946-7351
Website: https://www.sullivancountypa.gov

***

Susquehana County

Susquehanna County Courthouse
31 Lake Avenue
Montrose, PA 18801
Phone: (570) 278-4600
Website: https://www.susqco.com

***

Tioga County

Tioga County Courthouse
116 Main Street
Wellsboro, PA 16901
Phone: (717) 248-6733
Website: https://www.tiogacountypa.us

***

Union County

Union County Courthouse
103 South Second Street
Lewisburg, PA 17837
Phone: (570) 524-8762
Website: https://www.unioncountypa.org

***

Venango County

Venango County Courthouse
1168 Liberty Street
Franklin, PA 16323
Phone: (814) 432-9539
Website: https://www.co.venango.pa.us

***

Warren County

County of Warren
204 Fourth Avenue
Warren, PA 16365
Phone: (814) 728-3400
Website: https://warrencopa.com

***

Washington County

Washington County Courthouse
1 South Main Street
Washington, PA 15301
Phone: (724) 228-6806
Website: https://www.co.washington.pa.us

***

Wayne County

Wayne County Courthouse
925 Court Street
Honesdale, PA 18431
Phone: (570) 253-5970
Website: https://www.waynecountypa.gov

***

Westmoreland County

Westmoreland County Courthouse
2 North Main Street
Greensburg, PA 15601
Phone: (717) 248-6733
Website: https://www.co.westmoreland.pa.us

***

Wyoming County

Wyoming County Courthouse
1 Courthouse Square
Tunkhannock, PA 18657
Phone: (570) 836-3200
Website: https://wyomingcountypa.gov

***

York County

York County Archives
150 Pleasant Acres Road
York, PA 17402
Phone: (717) 840-7222
Website: https://www.yorkcountyarchives.org

York County Government
45 North George Street
York, PA 17401
Phone: (717) 771 - 9288
Website: https://yorkcountypa.gov

Appendix D: Archives with Historical Records

PENNSYLVANIA HAS HUNDREDS OF private, non-profit organizations around the state archiving historical records. The three largest private archives are listed here, along with the main historical and genealogical society for each county. These places do not hold the originals of government-issued vital records, for that see Appendix C. What they do have is indexes to the various vital records, and many of the substitutes for vital records listed in Chapter 10.

Genealogical and Historical Societies with Regional Collections

Genealogical Society of Pennsylvania
100 Byberry Road, Room 111
Philadelphia PA 19116
Website: www.genpa.org

Heinz History Center
1212 Smallman Street
Pittsburgh, PA 15222
Website: www.heinzhistorycenter.org

Historical Society of Pennsylvania
1300 Locust Street
Philadelphia, PA 19107
Website: www.hsp.org

North Eastern Pennsylvania Genealogical Society
57 North Franklin St,
Wilkes Barre PA 18701
Website: www.nepgs.com

Western Pennsylvania Genealogical Society
4400 Forbes Avenue
Pittsburgh, PA 15213
Website: www.wpgs.org

County Genealogical and Historical Societies

Adams County Historical Society
Website: www.achs-pa.org

Armstrong County Historical Museum and Genealogical Society, Inc.
Website: www.acmgs.org

Beaver County Genealogy & History Center
Website: www.bcgslibrary.org

Bedford County Historical Society
Website: www.bedfordpahistory.com

Berks County Genealogical Society
Website: www.berksgenes.org

Berks History Center
Website: www.berkshistory.org

Blair County Genealogical Society
Website: www.blairgenealogy.org

Bradford County Historical Society
Website: www.bradfordhistory.com

Bucks County Genealogical Society
Website: www.buckscountygenealogicalsociety.org

Butler Area Public Library, Weir Genealogy Room
Website: www.butlerlibrary.info/genealogy

Cambria County Historical Society
Website: www.cambriacountyhistorical.com

Cameron County Historical Society
Website: www.cameroncountyhistoricalsociety.com

Carbon County, Dimmick Memorial Library
Website: www.dimmicklibrary.org

Centre County Library and Historical Museum, The Pennsylvania Room
Website: www.centrecountylibrary.org/pennsylvania-room

Chester County Historical Society
Website: www.chestercohistorical.org

Clarion County Historical Society
Website: www.clarioncountyhistoricalsociety.org

Clearfield County Historical Society
Website: www.clearfieldcountyhistoricalsociety.org

Clinton County Historical Society
Website: www.clintoncountyhistory.com

Columbia County Historical and Genealogical Society
Website: www.columbiapahistory.com

Crawford County Historical Society
Website: www.crawfordhistorical.org

Cumberland County Historical Society
Website: www.historicalsociety.com

Historical Society of Dauphin County
Website: www.dauphincountyhistory.org

Delaware County Historical Society
Website: www.delcohistory.org

Elk County Historical Society
Website: www.elkcountyhistoricalsociety.org

Erie County Historical Society
Website: www.eriehistory.org

Erie Society for Genealogical Research
Website: www.esgr.org

Uniontown Library of Fayette County, Pennsylvania Room
Website: www.uniontownlib.org/pennsylvania-room

Fayette County Historical Society/Abel Colley Tavern & Museum
Website: www.fayettehistory.org

Forest County Historical Society
Website: www.forestcountyhistory.org

Franklin County Historical Society
Website: www.franklinhistorical.org

Franklin County Libraries, Coyle Free Library
Website: www.coylefreelibrary.org

Fulton County Historical Society Library, Genealogy Library
Website: www.fultonhistory.org

Cornerstone Genealogy Society of Greene County
Website: www.cornerstonegenealogy.com

Huntingdon County Historical Society, Genealogy Research Library
Website: www.huntingdonhistory.org

Historical and Genealogical Society of Indiana County
Website: www.rootsweb.ancestry.com/~paicgs

Jefferson County History Center
Website: www.jchconline.org

Juniata County Historical Society
Website: www.juniatacountyhistoricalsociety.org

Lackawanna Historical Society
Website: www.lackawannahistory.org

Lackawanna County Library, Albright Memorial Library
Website: www.lclshome.org/albright-memorial-library

Lancaster History, Archives and Special Collection Library
Website: www.lancasterhistory.org

Lawrence County Historical Society
Website: www.lawrencechs.com

Lebanon County Historical Society
Website: www.lebanoncountyhistoricalsociety.org

Lehigh Valley Heritage Museum & Archive
Website: www.lehighvalleyheritagemuseum.org

Luzerne County Historical Society
Website: www.luzernehistory.org

Osterhout Free Library of Luzerne County, Genealogy Collection
Website: www.osterhout.info/genealogy

Lycoming County Genealogical Society
Website: www.lycominglineage.org

Bradford Area Public Library of McKean County
Website: www.bradfordlibrary.org

Painted Hills Genealogy Society for McKean and Potter Counties
Website: www.paintedhills.org

Mercer County Historical Society
Website: www.mchspa.org

Mercer County Genealogical Society
Website: www.mercerheritage.org

Mifflin County Historical Society
Website: www.mifflincountyhistory.org

Eastern Monroe Public Library, Local History and Genealogy Room
Website: www.monroepl.org

Monroe County Historical Association
Website: www.monroehistorical.org

Historical Society of Montgomery County
Website: www.hsmcpa.org

Montour County Genealogical Society
Website: www.montourcountyhistoricalsociety.org

Easton Area Public Library, Marx Local History Room
Website: www.eastonpl.org

Northampton County Historical and Genealogical Society Archives
Website: www.northamptonctymuseum.org

Northumberland County Historical Society
Website: www.northumberlandcountyhistoricalsociety.org

The Perry Historians, Lenig Library
Website: www.perryhistorians.org

Pike County Historical Society
Website: www.pikecountyhistoricalsociety.org

Coudersport Public Library of Potter County
Website: www.coudersportlibrary.org

Potter County Historical Society
Website: www.pottercountypahistory.org

Schuylkill County Historical Society
Website: www.schuylkillhistory.org

Snyder County Historical Society
Website: www.snydercohistoricalsociety.org

Somerset Historical Center, Genealogical Research Library
Website: www.somersethistoricalcenter.org

Sullivan County Historical Society and Museum
Website: www.sullivancountyhistory.org

Susquehanna County Historical Society & Free Library Association
Website: www.susqcolibrary.org

Tioga County Historical Society
Website: www.tiogapahistory.org

Union County Historical Society
Website: www.unioncountypahistory.org

Franklin Public Library of Venango County, PA Room: Genealogy & Local History
Website: www.franklinlibrary.org

Oil City Public Library, Venango County Genealogical Club Collection
Website: www.oilcitylibrary.org

Warren County Historical Society
Website: www.warrenhistory.org

Warren County Public Library
Website: www.warrenlibrary.org

Citizens Library of Washington County, Genealogy Room
Website: www.citizenslibrary.org

Washington County Historical Society
Website: www.washcohistory.org

Wayne County Historical Society
Website: www.waynecountyhistory.com

Westmoreland History Education Center
Website: www.westmorelandhistory.org

Baltzer Meyer Historical Society for Westmoreland County
Website: www.baltzermeyer.com

Wyoming County Historical Society, Genealogical Library
Website: www.wyomingcountyhistoricalsociety.org

York County History Center, Library & Archives
Website: www.yorkhistorycenter.org

Appendix E: Additional Resources for Research

RESOURCES TO HELP WITH incorporating DNA results in research, learning historical boundaries, and working with variations in names.

DNA

A helpful resource for many genealogists is Roberta Estes website, *DNAeXplained*, **https://dna-explained.com**. Roberta provides resources for people who are in search of their biological family and people who have unexpected ancestors in their genetic family trees.

Foundational knowledge in DNA and its uses in genealogy research can be learned in Blaine Bettinger's *Genetic Genealogy in Practice*.

To learn methods to analyze DNA matches, the Family Locket book *Research Like a Pro with DNA* by Diana Elder, Nicole Dyer and Robin Wirthlin is highly recommended.

To jump right into methods of using DNA matches, Diahan Southard's book *Your DNA Guide the Book* will tell you exactly what to do.

County Boundary Changes

The majority of compulsory vital records occurred after Pennsylvania county boundary lines stabilized. But when tracing people prior to 1860, researchers will find Pennsylvania county lines changed frequently. People could have stayed in the same home their whole life, but the county they lived in changed two or three times. This matters because much of their life was conducted through the county courthouse. Two excellent free resources help determine the progression of county names and boundary lines:

- *The Pennsylvania Genealogical Map of the Counties* by the Pennsylvania Historical and Museum Commission at: **www.phmc.pa.gov/Archives/Documents/Pennsylvania-Genealogical-Map-Counties.pdf**.
- The Newberry Library's *Atlas of Historical County Boundaries* which gives exact calendar dates for the county changes: **https://digital.newberry.org/ahcb/pages/Pennsylvania.html**.

Given Names and Surnames

To understand varieties of given (first) names, this book is handy: *Nicknames Past and Present*, 5th edition, by Christine Rose

To determine origin of surname, an easy to use resource is *Behind the Name* **https://www.behindthename.com**

Irish Names

A book helpful for Irish and Scottish surnames: *The Book of Ulster Surnames*, by Robert Bell

For the frequency and spellings: *Irish Surname Maps* **https://www.barrygriffin.com/surname-maps/irish/**

German Names

To understand how pronunciation affected spelling from German to English, this is a great resource: "The Dialect Basis of Spelling Variation in German Surnames," *FamilySearch Wiki*, **https://www.familysearch.org/en/wiki/The_Dialect_Basis_of_Spelling_Variation_in_German_Surnames**

For the frequency and various spellings of German surnames: *Geogen* **http://geogen.stoepel.net**

To learn more about variations of German surnames: *Dictionary of German Surnames* **https://www.namenforschung.net/en/dfd/about-the-project/**

Americanization of Names and Occupations

Foreign Versions, Variations, and Diminutives of English Names; Foreign Equivalents of United States Military and Civilian Titles, by the U.S. Department of Justice, Immigration and Naturalization Service, 1973.

Sources

THE FOLLOWING SOURCES WERE used in creation of this book.

Laws of Pennsylvania, Harrisburg: Pennsylvania Government Printing, various years.

Busharis, Barbara J.; Dunn, Catharine M.; Tavares, Bonny L.; and Wale, Carla P.; *Pennsylvania Legal Research, Second Edition.* Durham, North Carolina: Carolina Academic Press, 2017.

Corbin, John, *Find the Law in the Library: A Guide to Legal Research.* Chicago: American Library Association, 1989.

Director, Robert M., *Guide to the Genealogical Sources at the Pennsylvania State Archives, 2nd Edition.* Harrisburg: Pennsylvania Historical and Museum Commission, 1998.

Eddy, Henry Howard, *The Guide to the Published Archives of Pennsylvania,* Harrisburg: Pennsylvania Historical and Museum Commission, 1949.

Greenwood, Val D., *The Researcher's Guide to American Genealogy, 4th Edition*. Baltimore: Genealogical Publishing Co., 2017.

Iscrupe, William L. and Iscrupe, Shirley G.M., *Pennsylvania Line: A Research Guide to Pennsylvania Genealogy and Local History, Fourth Edition.* Laughlintown, Pennsylvania: Southwest Pennsylvania Genealogical Services, 1990.

Livengood, Candy Crocker, *Genealogical Abstracts of the Laws of Pennsylvania and the Statues at Large.* Westminster, Maryland: Family Line Publications, 1990.

Pfeiffer, Laura Szucs, *Hidden Sources: Family History in Unlikely Places*. Orem, Utah: MyFamily.com, 2000.

Rose, Christine, *Courthouse Research for Family Historians: Your Guide to Genealogical Treasures, 2nd Edition*. San Jose, California: CR Publications, 2019.

Stevens, Sylvester K. and Kent, Donald H. , editors. *County Government and Archives in Pennsylvania.* Harrisburg: Pennsylvania Historical and Museum Commission, 1947.

Szucs, Loretto Dennis and Luebking, Sandra Hargreaves, editors. *The Source: A Guidebook to American Genealogy, 3rd ed*. Provo, Utah: Ancestry, 2006.

About the Author

DENYSE ALLEN IS THE founder of PA Ancestors L.L.C., a business centered on helping people discover their ancestors in Pennsylvania. Denyse's ancestors go back eight generations in Pennsylvania.

Denys has researched their lives in the courthouses and archives of Allegheny, Berks, Blair, Centre, Chester, Clearfield, Dauphin, Delaware, Lancaster, Montgomery, Northampton, Northumberland, Philadelphia, Schuylkill, Snyder, Union, and Westmoreland counties. This is Denyse's first book.

To learn about all that PA Ancestors offers, go to: **https://www.paancestors.com**

To receive the free newsletter covering a new genealogical records each week, go to **https://welcome.paancestors.com**

Book Bonuses

THIS BOOK COMES WITH bonus materials to help you with your genealogy research in Pennsylvania.

Download your bonuses from PA Ancestors, at **https://www.paancestors.com/book-bonuses/**.

To view a list of all of PA Ancestors genealogy books, go to **https://www.paancestors.com/books/**

For more help in your genealogy research, check out the following resource:

Free introduction to Pennsylvania genealogy course: **https://welcome.paancestors.com**

www.ingramcontent.com/pod-product-compliance
Lightning Source LLC
LaVergne TN
LVHW010618100826
845148LV00014B/3017

* 9 7 9 8 9 8 7 4 4 3 4 5 3 *